The 2022 Poetry Marathon Anthology

Edited by Ofuma Agali & Cristy Watson

Copyright 2023. All rights reserved to the respective authors.

ISBN: 978-1-942344-08-7

Cover image by Vidya Shankar

Contents

Full Marathon Introduction 7
Half Marathon Introduction 9

Full Marathon Poems 11
Gathering and Beating Inertia 13
Flashes from the Deep 29
Racing Against Pain 49
Tablets of Faith 59
Reality and the Elusive 79
Interlude of the Heartbeats 95
Morsels of Memories 119
Locomotive Locales 141
A Dip into Metaphors 152

Half Marathon Poems 163
Two Years On (And Still Counting) 165
Undone (Roe Vs. Wade and the Fallout) 173
Articulations (About our world... One another... Ourselves) 187
Lost... and Found (Liberties, Connections, Hope, Time) 233
Poetics (Poets, And the Art of Poetry) 293

Index of Poets 307

Full Marathon Introduction

Poetry finds deliberate expression in a community that is aware it has to write – waiting yearly to do just that, to unfasten buckled words, to sink into the ocean of extempore, and to swim in the adjoining sea – fed by each poet's river, floating in the words that emerge. And from the multiple harvests of expressions, this anthology furnishes its home with these consequent selected poems. "We will cast our nets and catch the words/…carrying with us for one whole year/the exhilaration of swimming in the poet's river," Anjana Sen notes in her poem.

117 poems of diverse forms now inhabit the full marathon section of this anthology. There has been a technically-imperfect but conscious effort to split these poems into nine sections with random roots in The writer's effort, Poetic flashes of here and beyond, Pain, Faith, Elusiveness, Pleasure, Memories, Locale, and The metaphorical. From these poems, we find lines that wink, twinkle, frown, smile, ululate, and also those that drip with immense joy and biting sorrow.

"All of my oceans are waking/filling my body with currents," Sandra Duncan writes. "The body wails, the mind antagonizes/Excruciating comfort silences all," Renee A. Perkins laments. Joshua Factor expresses gratitude "…for being a light in a world fueled by darkness. "Where did our innocence go?" Chidi Nebo questions. Cynthia Hernandez's line, "I sipped joy all morning," brightens the poet's day. David Bruce Patterson reminds of memories that live, "tasting a part of" us. Margo Wilson's translocation of "a Garden of Eden" into her "backyard" reignites the poet's migration deposits, all withdrawn in words. Carol Prost tells of "ruby lips" that drip "summer's feast in the magic of moonlight."

These lines often take flight, exporting the reader into "other" spaces and otherness; they also stay rooted, forcing the reader to erect a nest in the poet's world. In the midst of these free and experimental forms, we also find fine efforts in gigan, sonnet, zuhitsu, villanelle, and so on. You may find that a few lines might throw you off track, but you will also find yourself landing safely in the basket of poetic license.

For good measure, this collection also reveals a community of poets who still harbor memories of the pandemic, but who are consciously moving away from the emotional trap into the worlds ahead – one filled with conflicting uncertainties with perhaps only the poet's feet taking certain steps. It has indeed been a delight to work with the organizers of this global poetry festival – Caitlin and Jacob, the community of participants, and my co-editor, Cristy, in the creation of this work. Do go ahead and feast on the words, harvested on a platter of muses.

Ofuma Agali

Half Marathon Introduction

"Poetry is the lifeblood of rebellion, revolution, and the raising of consciousness."

~Alice Walker

Because of its ability to bring people together, the Poetry Marathon has played an important role in connecting poets over the past years, and during the Pandemic, especially as we slowly emerge from our homes and make our way back into society. Along with Caitlin and Jacob Jans, poets from around the world have created a community over these past years that has had a pivotal and sustaining influence during Covid.

Maybe being sequestered for long periods of time, and more cautious these past two years, has also given us ample opportunities for reflection and quiet moments to think about recent injustices in our world and to become even more appreciative of our planet. As poets, we have always written about these things, but now, more people are listening.

After reading the 244 poems submitted to the half-marathon, similar themes emerged in our collective struggles during Covid, our strong feelings toward violations of human rights occurring across our lands, and our fierce love for Nature and one another. These brilliant poems captured the human condition, in all its glory and despair; with our words helping to challenge perspectives, and to remind us of everything that connects us to one another.

Continue to raise up your voices! For it is through poetry, that we see and know ourselves.

Half-Marathon Editor,

Cristy Watson

Full Marathon

Gathering and Beating Inertia

"O! for a muse of fire, that would ascend the brightest heaven of invention."

William Shakespeare

Anjana Sen
Glasgow, Scotland, United Kingdom
Hour 1

The Poet's River

And so, it starts. After being poised, quivering
in nervous anticipation, shivering.
Prompt on the hour, the claxon sounds.
As one, we pinch noses, dive in, from separate grounds.

Safe. Knowing as I do, I'll be underwater with you
for the next twenty-four hours. The day (and night), only ours,
to gently swim together, or race.
To frolic, glide, discover – at our own pace.

We will cast our nets and catch the words
attached to everything everywhere like seaweed.
We will string them together into verse,
which we will wonder over later as we read.

I'll remain fresh, calm, joyous and still.
And when I flag, for flag and flail I will,
you will nudge me, not judge me. Or let me bail out.
I'll waken from exhaustion as I hear you shout.

As will I, for you, my brethren, my tribe so dear,
I'll say bravo as often as you want to hear.
And together we will string the pearls of words into verses.
And send them out bravely, into the universe.

Once the day is done, then the night, then the day again, bright,
we will start swimming up towards the light.
Reach up. Break water. Gasp at the shock of the glare.
Shake off the droplets of exhaustion. Breathe in air,

carrying with us for one whole year
the exhilaration of swimming in the poet's river.

Amanda Potter
Jacksonville, Florida
Hour 4

The Poetry Marathon

Once a year we gather
worldwide
connected by the internet and Wi-Fi

Armed with our tools
fingers that strike keys
pens that bleed ink

we shed our words
these thoughts and feelings
memories reeling

 exposing our seams
through this poetic community

We hold space
for what was, hoping
for what comes

yearning to be seen
longing to be read.

What we mark
between the lines
is what we poets love

Jessica Leanne Gershon
Covington, Tennessee
Hour 6

A Poet's Dream

Take me back to the old days
where my soul had just begun,
all the way to the end of time,
that's where my heart will run;
I will not be contained,
do not put me in a box.
My body will feel the pain,
but my soul will not.
Sprinkle my ashes in the morning,
watching the sun rise,
spending no time mourning;
my love never dies.
The circle of life you see,
in the golden hour of ups and downs,
that's where I will be,
making bird sounds.
Listen to your heart,
hear the music of the birds;
our souls are true art,
what we see are the words.

Janis Martin
Dorset, United Kingdom
Hour 12

Gathering

In times of uncertainty
I seek out The Others
gathered together
at the usual place
easily recognizable
by the colours they wear
There's no ceremony
ritual or secret passwords
Just a place to gather
to seek support
and understanding from friends
Questions carefully teased apart
worked through and debated
An opportunity to share
and care about one another
Familiar faces, welcoming embraces
laughter or tears
joy or mutual fears
But that's why we gather
To show we belong
Each of us here
are part of The Others

Ofuma Agali
Lagos, Nigeria
Hour 24

The Muse ii

In that blurry kingdom of inspiration,

muses are trapped in coloured bottles
where grain alcohol transports them onto blank pages.

These muses dance on the slippery pages,
making efforts to stick, to be counted, and be read.

Sometimes, the birthed words fly into the eyes of the drinker
who then shakes off catapulted confusion by seeking the bottle once more.

Paper balls, cracked pen stems, and white spaces adorn.
In a sane minute or two, a sensible chord is struck
in that cloud of dust where clarity is ephemeral.

It might be great art to gamble with muses resident in a bottle;
perhaps not the thought that they live anywhere at all, muses!

Cindy Albers
Wailuku, Maui, Hawaii
Hour 22

I Need an Idea, Not Tenderness

I need an idea
to reach out and grab me,
shake me awake,
pull me out of dreamland,
bring me back to the almost-alive,
an idea to pull me back from the precipice.
I need an idea,
something to fly with, drive with
or at the very least cry with,
an idea I can sink my teeth into,
throw in some words,
some sentence structure,
and mix them all up.
Just one small idea,
something, anything at all,
toss me a word, a generality,
a token or a snippet maybe;
just not the word "tenderness"
that won't do it.
I need something less soft,
more word-worthy.
I need powerful poetry.

Catherine Dickson
Georgia
Hour 9

Drive-Thru Poetry

Sometimes the words come
like the bubbles in a McDonald's Sprite,
effervescently effortless and
wholly unstoppable.
But most of the time,
the words are like a jar of jam,
whose lid has been glued stuck
in a saccharine crust,
cemented in the chill
of the fridge door.
Hands sweaty, clenched jaw,
gasping in outlandish shock
that they would dare
resist command.
Sometimes I can find
the things to say,
but mostly,
the words are like that.

Cindy Thompson
Lakewood, Colorado
Hour 8

At the Soda Shoppe

The poem sits coyly at the counter of the Soda Shoppe,
waiting to be discovered, slowly sipping an egg cream.
Making it last all day, the creamy lukewarm liquid
drips down its poetically pointed chin,
a sticky puddle forming at its iambic feet.
The Soda Shoppe's bell tinkles;
a thirsty reader breathlessly arrives.
Taking a stool next to the poem, she reaches over and lifts the creation to her lips.
Tasting its invigorating words, she sucks down its essence of life, grins and leaves.
Reveling in being discovered,
the poem sits coyly at the counter of the Soda Shoppe.
The Soda Shoppe's bell tinkles.
In the throes of a moon-in-June love quarrel, a young couple enters.
Sitting on the other side of the poem, they decry the sticky mess on the floor.
Dripping with the dregs of saccharine philosophy, the poem chuckles,
"It's so sad when uncultured people don't realize what delights are just within reach."

Ekawu Elizabeth Imaji
Abuja, Nigeria
Hour 16

By Mouthing the Memories of a Mowed Nightmare

A poem counts everything living as a memory
and tries on different shapes to fit into its body.
First, she squeezes into boy;
a boy trying the figure of a sea,
a sea too little to hold the sins of his past as secret,
a secret too thick, it could suffocate his own Mother.
Then, this same boy becomes dead even before he has the opportunity to live.
He is silent even before the lips
finds a smooth note for speech,
and he is choking even before plunging on a memory.
How can a boy die before life breathes inside of him?
Remember, this is just a poem,
the one counting everything living
as a memory,
and tries on different shapes to fit into its body.

Nandiya Nyx
Philadelphia, Pennsylvania
Hour 2

On Writing, with appreciation to Robert Frost

Of easy wind and downy flake
I cast a line my heart to wake
And though it quakes with awesome fury
The pen holds fast, most securely.
The only other sound's the sweep
The scratchy scrawl, as words do leap
The truth it's hooked, as soul demands
I reel it in, the poem here lands.

*First line of each stanza taken from Robert Frost's "Stopping by Woods on a Snowy Evening"

Sincerely BlueJay
Las Vegas, Nevada
Hour 9

Crystalized Adoration

If you hold this on your tongue
and let it dissolve like a fresh fallen
snowflake two days before your birthday,
you will engrain this taste into your memory.

The ink will flow from you freely and often,
the story will be yours to tell any time you like,
and the poetry will morph so flawlessly with the
creatures and art you surround yourself with,
that you may even begin to forget who created what.

I like to think that if you hold this idea
on your tongue for long enough you will
almost never be able to forget what my
poetry and I tasted like either.

Megan Dausch
New York
Hour 4

Rain

Raindrops tap the world.
Hands on a keyboard. Watering;
unfolding stories.

Abena Ntoso
Houston, Texas
Hour 24

Finish Lines

crossing, i commence
a commitment to carrying
all that i have brought
wrought thought
it's clearly the end of the hours
and while i haven't bought flowers
i would not say of anyone in the world now
that they wrote this or wrote that
as we dozed and stumbled
finished lines we may or may not keep
in the revision which begins with crossing

Flashes from the Deep

"From the ashes a fire shall be woken, A light from the shadows shall spring."

J.R.R. Tolkien

Samantha Carroll
South Carolina
Hour 1

Into the Clouds

Storm clouds come rolling in,
Waiting for the downpour with bated breath, tongue tied.
Let the rain drown out the pain.

Into the clouds now,
don't make a sound.
The rain lives in her veins.
The ocean is alive in her eyes.
The water pours from her soul.

She was born of water,
not just someone's daughter,
lost to the hurricane alive in her soul.
The rain within her never leaves her alone.

Fall into the clouds now.
Stop! Don't make a sound.
The rain is alive inside.
The ocean calls her home.
The water comes from her very soul.

Lee Montgomery-Hughes
North Ayrshire, Scotland, UK
Hour 1

The Call of the Sea

When shall I go down to the sea again,
to the salty sea and the waves?
When will my desire be fulfilled,
to taste the air I crave?

When will I answer the questions
waves ask lapping at my feet?
What is the draw of the ocean
and why does my heart miss a beat
when I hear the cry
of the gulls on high
as I watch the water play
and wonder at the tall ships passing by?

Will I ever go down to the sea again,
taste the salt and smell the breeze?
When will my life-long desire be fulfilled
and my soul once again be at ease?

Sandra Duncan
Portland, Victoria, Australia
Hour 8

I am ocean

All my oceans are waking,
filling my body with currents,

replacing the blood in my veins,
rushing through my miles
so rapidly, I wave as I walk.

I hunger for raw fish and seaweed,
for the smell of salty air.

The moon is my master now;
I follow her night and day,
I have become her wild young slave.

All my oceans are waking.
I hunger for raw fish and seaweed.

Given Davis
Portland, Oregon
Hour 1

Amphibious

I was a small thing
watching the shifty line
between ocean and sand
a changing place
where I could find home
tides pulling under
the loose earth
of my body

Below the surface
it was quiet
I held my breath
as she rocked me
lulled by her heartbeat

Waking on my back
a flock of nurses in white
floated through the room

When I came out of surgery
my first breaths were shallow

I was born in the ocean
taking my first steps
on land

Ashley "LuvMiFreely" Powers
Dayton, Ohio
Hour 7

Under The Surface

This growing pressure
that choking feeling in my throat
I feel it all building up in my chest
my emotions at its breaking point
My outer appearance shows no sign of damage
Not one crack present
Can't allow myself to shatter
I'm the strong one
Ash, keep it together
I'm ready to fold
Expectations high and failure isn't an option
I'm forced to carry this load
I buckle and bend
But somehow I don't break
I guess I was made to handle any burden
take on any fate
Although I take what I'm handed and never question it
doesn't mean it's not heavy
and that it isn't weighing on my spirit
I've conditioned myself to smile
But under the surface I'm drowning

Eilidh St John
Albany, Western Australia
Hour 21

Circles

In my arms life ebbs
Not away but into more
Birth and death unite

Lesley Tyson
Reston, Virginia
Hour 8

coincidence

i never thought of this place as small
so our meeting was a cosmic coincidence

except our erratic orbits sometimes
circle the same planets at times
marked in different slants of light

we teach each other different idioms
strange modifications of a single root

we carefully clear the debris of our baggage
of our origins to find degrees of separation

we remember echoes of a voice saying
i never thought of this place as small

we teach each other different idioms
to explain opposite sides of legends
that we will not complete

that task will fall to the historians
and the characters they create

Tracy Plath
Franklin, Indiana
Hour 8

Waning

My adult womanly existence is flush with the full moon;
a Super Moon when closest to my earthly focus, my love,
a Micro Moon when distant, small and dull in the dark.

Wolves keened my loneliness in the cold Wolf Moon,
the Snow Moon marked my February birth.

A Blood Moon's rarity radiated red, brought forth little deaths of youth,
shed uterine linings prepared my womb for new life.

Blue Moon, you marked my sons' entrances into the world,
and the Pink Moon of soft Spring gave both life and death to my twin girls.

Strawberry Moon, I believed I would forever be fertile, vibrant,
my adult womanly existence flush with the full moon.

Blood on the moon radiated red, brought forth the death of first love,
but the Buck Moon gifted a richer love in the full flush of summer,
the Corn Moon's harvest gave me his heart.

Frost Moon, I am waning, my woman's blood drying.
Long Nights Moon, one night soon, I will lay me down.

Viswo Varenya Samal
Keonjhar, Odisha, India
Hour 24

Denouement

Evening of life
waiting at the doorway
primrose oil lamp burns
scarlet flames rise unwittingly
embracing the lovely evening

Deborah Lynn Dalton aka D², @d2poetry
Charlotte, North Carolina
Hour 17

Pulled the Trigger

Take up

in casual conversation
a
scenario is described
innocently
raising alarm

Break

the words stayed
in my head
days later
and would swim
in my mind
bouncing
without conscious purpose
until it connected

Overtravel

and then the spin
noticeable
and uncontrollable
at moments
sparking irrational behavior
running ram shod on routines
and plans
goals seem so foreign

Reset

once recognized
grappling to unwind
pull the crazy back on the spool
and confront what was unbound

Momo Campbell
California
Hour 3

Beneath the Hangman's Tree

A man stood beneath the tree,
waiting it seemed, for me.
His gaze was soft as diamond,
his mood as light as iron,
he had been waiting for me;
but why beneath this tree?

This tree was like most around it,
red leaves and branches.
But unlike boughs in woods confounded,
this one stood alone,
the hangman's noose upon its branch,
the grass around it dead.
And though I felt fit as a fiddle,

the tree filled me with dread.

I approached the man with care.
He asked me for my name,
perhaps trying to cause a scare.
He asked my silence again;
at last I felt my courage rise
and deigned it wise to answer
and he nodded, to my surprise,

he Spoke. "Born the sign of cancer"

How could he know that, I did wonder.
Then realization dawned.
This was no man, nor land I lived in.
My life, indeed, was gone.
The memory threatened to drown me
but He then took my hand.
I left there as Death had found me
and guided my soul to the promised land.

River E. Styx
Bangor, Maine
Hour 3

Untitled

I don't plan on having arthritic bones to dig up.
No anthropologist will have to wonder
if my hips belonged to a boy or a girl.
Instead, they will be the taproot;
My ribs opened into a tree.
A strong oak whose branches reach for the morning sun.
Leaves eat up every last drop
while my canopy offers solace.
Cellulose stronger than my collagen ever dreamed of being.
Squirrels will forget where they buried acorns
made of my memories.
Birds will build their nests with the remains of my heart.
My failures won't matter after I nourished this tree— fed this forest.
I don't care who remembers me
so long as the forest still whispers my name.

Fiona Ryle
Fort Frances, Ontario, Canada
Hour 21

Gumdrop Acapella

gumdrops fall, like rain
bouncing off my umbrella
singing acapella

cotton candy threads fly by
almonds glide and hop
will they never stop?

red and black liquorice strands
dance around the square
like Rogers and Astaire

that sure was some dream
think i better stay away
from sriracha and Bublé

Sara Anderson
Franklin, Indiana
Hour 21

Soggy Shoes

Yellow umbrella
tugged from my hands suddenly,
soars on storming wind.

Ermelinda Makkimane
Goa, India
Hour 15

veins

delicate veins
that throb no more
still calm in their
fragility
perfect poise
even in death
and dying

Torri Brown
Tacoma, Washington
Hour 23

Loves Executioner

Around here
I survive off very little affection
Judgement begins in the eyes
It brings with it the possibility of being nothing
I choose to process life alone
with less intrusion
from the outside
I desire to be personified in love
without sacrificing my sensitivity
to break

Jade Walker
Chicago, Illinois
Hour 4

Mathematical Thoughts

Thoughts.
Like irrational numbers,
endlessly whining,
often never pausing
to take a break;

and cannot be broken,
like zero cannot be divided.

The only hope is
Logic.

Silvester Phua
North Vancouver, British Columbia, Canada
Hour 1

Endless

Floating on a dead sea,
one with eternity.
The world disappears,
along with all fears.
At twilight's dusk,
peace, alone, at last.

Racing Against Pain

"The pain, it will leave once it has finished teaching you."

Pavana Reddy

Renee A. Perkins
Washington, District of Columbia
Hour 9

Woe

Sorrow raptures;
its delicate waves froth enticingly toward the woebegone,
simmering beneath the frightful waters.
Woe, woe, it calls. Aching menace, it calls.
Where is our hope?
We cling to our sorrow; we strain for the waters.
Lurking deep, it sings its song.
Woe, woe.

Waters beckon.
Promises of lethe.
Promises of death.
Where is our future?
Weakened bones crack.
The body shrieks its defiance. It is not a willing submit.
But the mind, oh the mind!
Woe, woe.

Sorrow shatters,
gripped in harrowing claws.
No hope, no future.
The body wails, the mind antagonizes.
Excruciating comfort silences all.
Shuddering throes, stuttering beats,
enveloped in sorrowed waters.
Woe, woe.

Ian Barkley
Carbondale, Illinois
Hour 6

The Personal is Political

Open the blinds to let the light in for the first time in a long time.
Apartment windows across the parking lot,
background processes, gadgets, holy books, and dust,
three white walls and a fan that hums
forever, burning fuel like a living, temporary thing,
pushing away oppressive heat or cold.
Information overload and understimulation,
sound and failing vision,
everything you are
sinks into a screen that replaces
everything real
as the rest of the world retreats.
Thoughts get dark and fantasy becomes a need.
Deprivation leads to a blind and reckless hunger.

Michelle Adegboro
Nigeria
Hour 24

Pronouncing S.O.S

and i gazed afloat nature,
only to find the carcass of this broken body.

who says there is hope?
find me cure,
for this body is hollow.

i wish to ignite a poem,
besides this sagging body.

say, i might just pass out the pain
by clouding my heart with strings of your hands.

look, my humanity is ablaze,
i am drowning in doom's silence.

just breathe a sign towards
my destination

and tell me
i would not drown in these waters,

and I gazed afloat nature.

Natasha Vanover
Seattle, Washington
Hour 3

The State of Our Here and Now

Guns have more rights than women's wombs.
Death is more lauded than life.
Funerals are becoming more prevalent than nuptials.
Hospice hurts while hospitals no longer heal.
A father's love cannot be valued in conventional currency.
The sky offers more hope than any book.
A simple hello or message out of the blue is more far reaching than a new declaration of love.
The smile of a child can wash all your worries almost instantaneously.
Music is more meaningful than any promise presumes to be.
The sun's energetic embrace is more uplifting than any tangible want one can imagine.
Transferring sound, thoughts, dreams, and prayer into the spoken word is as powerful as putting them to paper, if not more.
We have now entered a holy realm when we speak aloud our needs, acknowledging the chasm in between.
As diverse as the opposite ends of the color spectrum,
both call out to be acknowledged, not necessarily accepted, only heard.
They too need a voice to give way to the sacred space that everyone can enter.
Come home to the here and now that only you can liberate.

Deanna Ngai
Airdrie, Alberta, Canada
Hour 15

Ghost Leaves

Ghost leaves stirring on the trees,
shifting in the gentle breeze.
A brittle reminder before the freeze
of the winter that is to come.

Early in the year they were green,
bright and vibrant, oh so clean,
shimmering with a fragile sheen,
pristine in spring.

As fall creeped in, they slowly turned,
lazily, not so concerned,
losing the colour they had learned,
turning into ghost leaves.

Amy Laird
Spencer, Iowa
Hour 12

Jonah

I've left God on hold
for far too long-
Started to pray,

only to tell him
that I'd be right back
and never came back.

I wonder why
he sticks around.
It's not like I make him
a priority-
Except for the obvious,

when things go wrong,
when I need prayer,
when there's a death
or simply when I feel wronged.

Why is that?

Anytime I call out,
he's there.
Anytime my life is in danger,
he's there.
Anytime I need something,
you guessed it,
he's there.

I'm sorry God;
I'm a horrible human being,
selfish,
obnoxious,
toxic,
unworthy of love and respect,
just-
Unworthy.

I don't understand how or why
you love me,
how others love me,
how they care for me,
it annoys and angers me
sometimes.

Do you do well to be so angry,
my little crab?

What was that?
I swear I hear someone
saying I have no right to
be angry.
But that can't be true.

I'll pay it no mind;
It doesn't matter
other people's opinions-
Of course, I do well
to be angry.
It is my right.

I'm just going to leave
it here and see what happens.
I have my comfort and my needs
are met.
But something's lacking.

Do you do well to be angry,
my little crab?
I'll ask you once more,
answer me.

I have a RIGHT to be angry.
I turned my back and she
threw me out on the sidewalk.
Who does that?

Tablets of Faith

"Faith is an oasis in the heart which will never be reached by the caravan of thinking."

Khalil Gilbran

Vidya Shankar
Chennai, India
Hour 24

Faith

viboothi[1]. no believer in amulets and the kind, this plain-looking ash is my only solace

i stand under the shower allowing the water to hug me. the sprays pierce through my skin, rejuvenating weary cells. i am aware of worry dissolving, layer by layer. i soap myself vigorously so i can peel more of them

fresh clothes are always cathartic. so is fresh skin

i light the evening lamp. its glow, soft yet powerful, roots me to the moment. i take a pinch of viboothi between my forefinger and thumb, and chanting a strotra[2], apply it to my forehead. no believer in amulets and the kind, this plain-looking ash is my only solace

the challenge begins. so does my journey

plod... plod...

is the journey a challenge or the challenge a journey?

surprisingly, i don't feel drained. is it because i am focused?

plod... plod...

plod... plod... and then, something magical happens. a shift. all is well again

the evening lamp shines on. no believer in amulets and the kind, this plain-looking ash is my only solace

sprinkles of stardust

viboothi

1. sacred ash used in Hindu rituals, it is often worn on the forehead as a reminder that there is a greater energy force in the universe and so one must try to practice detachment and be less egoistical.

2. (in Hinduism) a hymn written in praise of the Almighty

Joshua Factor
Durham, North Carolina, USA
Hour 11

Satellite

Home away from home,
perhaps a tad cliche but nothing if not accurate.
With the most incredible architecture and an unmatched ambience,
it's no mystery why it's the best getaway imaginable.

The alcove comes complete with delectable cuisine,
personal pods for unique consumption as you see fit,
and connectivity that has to be experienced to be believed.

When everything goes wrong, it's always here.
When the world seems to be falling to pieces,
it's a comforting refuge for the weary and indigent.
A single point of consistency in a perpetually changing world
with cartesian coordinates of zero zero zero zero.

Long after we're gone, it will remain for future generations to appreciate
but our perpetual, undying love and gratitude will remain long after
the end of time and the collapse of civilization.

Thanks for being a light in a world fueled by darkness.

Roxann Lawrence
Negril, Jamaica
Hour 9

Future Reflections

Just a glimmer.
The light is yet to be born,

preparing for tomorrow
when yesterday is gone.

When will the light be present?
When truths will be revealed,
will there be gladness
when those needs are healed?

Many are the questions
future promises bring.
When sunlight shines through darkness,
birds begin to sing.

This future reflection,
beaming wonder, poise and grace,
as you smell the beauty shone,

it sends a bright smile on your face

Rarzack Olaegbe
Lagos, Nigeria
Hour 18

Pure ecstasy

Waiting can be painful
if you aren't sure of the reason
you are in the prison
for the season.

The moment you know
and you can see,
it is pure ecstasy,

like an unfruitful couple
gifted with twin diamonds
after twenty years.

Aishwarya Vedula
Bilaspur, Chhattisgarh, India
Hour 15

Moonchild

On a night full of stars,
I drink wine stirred by the flowers.

I raise my glass offering a glass to moon,
and noticed my shadow holding the same.

The gentle sensation of seclusion down the throat,
softening the syllables of every word uttered;

seeking the slices of the moon,
on a table covered with upholstery planets.

Angel Rosen
Pittsburgh, Pennsylvania
Hour 1

Meeting Myself in the Chesapeake Bay

I did leave something in the estuary last Friday.
It wasn't a wrinkled dollar bill,
miserably wet in my swimsuit pocket.
It wasn't a soggy pizza crust, now departed.

The ugly brown water took from me,
a section of sadness
that it later will turn into salt.
My tears making a transition
into ocean, and I
into invincible—
imagining myself as a child
for a single moment,
doggy-paddling towards
the sun tucked into the water beside me,
resembling a breakfast hash brown.

I will get there, I think.
The water can't take me,
but I can take myself.

Sandra Johnson
Houston, Texas
Hour 21

Emotion Eggs

In a clear, small caddy,
emotion eggs they sit,
each one makes the eater feel
the feeling face on it.

Should I choose the first one,
frazzled, scrambled in both ends?
Second, worried, like I get
when itchy rash won't mend.

Third, I like the very most
happy, sun side up;
next one, scared eyes wide
maybe jalapeños inside,
I dare not touch that pup.

The back row, I can imagine now
sad, shocked and sick, and how
that one's uncooked, and pallid,
never in mouth be swallowed.

The very last emotion, angering,
this one's blown out, yolk strings dangling,
need this one when phone is ringing
unknown call, confront some spamming.

I'd love to share emotion eggs,
they may just come in handy;
love-peace omelettes I'd give the world
'til together we're just dandy.

Renata Pavrey
Mumbai, India
Hour 18

Happy Feet

Ghunghroos wound around ankles
like fairy dust sprinkled on my feet
magic swirling its way up and around
paying homage to Mother Earth

The soft caress of a silk saree
adorned with silver jewellery
on my neck, waist, arms
wearing headgear like a crown

The dance is a gift
for dancer and audience
more than a prayer
or choreography

Hands and feet painted with alta
I am a creation of color
through my dance, I bring
hope and happiness

Heart bursting with joy
at doing what I love
sharing a story through
music, movement, rhythm

I'm happiest when I dance
on stage and off it
feet nestled in ghunghroos

fairy dust guiding every step

K. L. Vivian
Houston, Texas
Hour 15

After the Drought

All gentleness is gone,
shriveled, curled and peeling in flakes.

The air holds dust so light it becomes a color,
stifling the landscape.
It never falls.

We breathe it and our lungs choke with loss.
Nothing can shine.
Everywhere green hope lies gasping.

There is a quiet pain, always just beyond awareness
until a sharp, angular light pierces the sullen haze
like a fierce intensity of longing
for the lost and unattainable.

My body lies parched like a gaping mouth
straining for breath, unable to moisten
its cracked lips. Choked.

Limp arms flail meaninglessly, and life
leaks out of a heart crusted over.

You arrive like the first drops of a long, sweet rain.

Leonora Obed
Ewing Township, New Jersey
Hour 3

My Big Dipper Helmet

I am waiting to be born.
Squatting on the welcome mat
of the world,
I mimic my bullfrog totem
animal
and croak and burp and fart.
But no attempt
can match his majesty.
My bullfrog jumps on my head and creates
a halo of mud and slime above and around
my eyebrows,
a taste of what's to come.
He starts the chorus
and I pretend to be a coqui,
the Caribbean crooner
exiled to a Hawaiian luau.
I am impatient,
wanting so much to be born.
I want to jump onto the sea of stars
and fall into the Big Dipper's
domain.
My body's heavy.
My head even heavier.
Bullfrog says my parents have seen my huge head
and
return me to God.
I don't know it yet,
but
no more of me will be born,
ever.
I'm a Down's Syndrome Child
and I wear my Star-Helmet
with Pride.

Katie Scholan
Bristol, United Kingdom
Hour 12

May Morning

They amass to raise the sun,
the ropes a braid of chord and song,
the darkness folk to cheer them on
as through the night they gather on.

In the starlight, start to weave
a netting out of ringing feet,
and momentarily believe
as the shout goes up to 'heave!'

First light like a banner pale;
a gauzy dawn, perhaps too frail?
To lift the weight of summer's sail,
but never do the dancers fail.

As she mounts into the air,
unimaginable pennants flare;
amber, gold and yet more rare,
to celebrate this cosmic care.

They amass to raise the sun,
their ropes a braid unfailing strong,
of love and hope and dance and song.
And though they laugh to move along,

they will be back again, ere long.

Donna Meyer
West Virginia
Hour 18

Fragments

A window shatters
Tiny squares of glass cascade down
mixing with the gravel in my driveway
bright and unnatural as diamonds

For days I sift through the gravel
my gloved hand picking out cuboids
and prisms and oblongs and shards
separating shiny window glass from the dusty gravel

I picture myself as Cinderella
picking the lentils from the ashes
What a tedious task that was

But it is not so bad
here on my front step
Dustpan full of gravel
Bucket filling with glass

Like Cinderella
I have the birds to sing to me

Mark Lucker
Minneapolis, Minnesota
Hour 21

Practicality

"Come in, she said I'll give ya shelter from the storm."
– Bob Dylan

I have never had much use
for umbrellas
keeping rain at bay
as antithetical
to a poet as
sunscreen to a snowman
I need no stick-canopy
except for thoughts
let it rain, pour
in my words you'll find
shelter
from your storm

Megan McDonald
Fairfax, Virginia
Hour 8

On the Edge

the walkers on the edge
balance the turns

they are the stilt walkers
chair builders
aerial ribbon weavers

they make joy out of chaos
make mundane magical

the audience watches
the impossible done daily

when the impossible flies
the walkers on the edge

are the transition from tricks to magic
when reality fades

magic is born
making joy out of chaos

Angela L Pantilione
Scottsdale, Arizona
Hour 1

Hush of morning

From the rush comes the hush of the morning
where the birds continue to sing above the din
as the traffic hustles and bustles
with roaring cars going nowhere
to places they will never remember.

The pool stands still as the planes fly over
reflecting their flight into the unknown.
The coolness of the morning quietly carries
birdsong causing the pool to ripple…
still though– undisturbed by the clamoring of man.

Mourning doves softly coo and coo, lamenting the world
while the finches figure out ways
to drink from the depths of the pool.
The Kingbird trills as the traffic builds.
And the Mockingbirds mimic all.

Aditi Dixit
Lucknow, India
Hour 17

I may not be The Best

In this world full of charms,
I may not be the best;
yet certainly, I'm not like the rest,
a path wide enough
for only two of us to walk abreast.
The feelings the emotions,
no real love, just the lust,
failed to learn the maneuvers,
mocked by the dirty trickers
trying to kill my innocence,
every action under a surveillance,
trying to overcome the resentment.
Ignored the Prophecy,
fallen prey to Destiny,
it's not as easy as I assumed
to conserve the world from being doomed.
I guess I was wrong;
fixing the cold world,
filling the warmth of love
is not going to be easy as a task.
Yet, I am happy with the suffering;
the cost I paid for honesty is vast.
In this world full of fallacies,
I may not be the best,
but at least I am not like the rest.

Joyce Bugbee
Higganum, Connecticut
Hour 22

Tenderness

Tenderness
a feeling
an emotion

Tenderness
soft
gentle

Tenderness
grandma's hands
mom's kiss

Tenderness

Reality and the Elusive

"Either you deal with what is the reality, or you can be sure that the reality is going to deal with you."

Alex Haley

Gabby Gilliam
North Potomac, Maryland
Hour 16

Still Here but Buried Deep

I was wild strawberries in a Tupperware bowl,
taste of summer sun and sweetness on tongue.

I was bare feet running on gravel,
thick-skinned from habit and determination.

I was warm milk in a bucket and hay-filled hair,
practiced hands unafraid to jump from the loft.

I was pine sap and climbing to the highest branch,
tough to wash off but appreciative of the view.

Where did that confident girl go?

Chidi Nebo
Lagos, Nigeria
Hour 1

Rain

childhood is but a distant past,
when we flaunted our naked innocence
before a dying world,
shrieking at the silvery darts
dotting our bodies with pimples of rain.

now the rain is gone;
the rainbow of life gradually fades
like our innocence
and on our dried-out lips the question hangs-
where did our innocence go?

DS Coremans
Stirling, Scotland
Hour 1

Life is Art

Does art imitate life, or is life art?
A sequence of exhibits to be seen
just once in a lifetime, or through a screen
but beauty feels superficial through glass.

Only by standing with bare feet upon the grass
can you understand what feeling must mean
to the birds on the branches as they preen
...birds which were ready to fly from the start.

It is in their nature to touch the sky;
to return, to build a home from debris,
creating new life without intention.
Nature is beauty; without having to try
or be shown, birds build a nest in a tree
making it ready for their creation.

J. Lynn Turney
Huntsville, Ontario, Canada
Hour 1

The Pleasure of Dipping Toes

Golden, velvet, sloping sand,
an invitation
to a conversation ongoing as life.

Feeling it through my toes
long before touching the fluttering, fluid edges,
cool and damp, assuring you're there.

Crossing the line between land to sea,
hesitant, polite and respectful,
gentle waves tickle, tempting memories to the surface.

"I've been here before,"
I sigh at the connection.
Whispering with each lap, you reply,
"Forever, so have I."

Starla Tipton
Mandan, North Dakota
Hour 19

luminescence

a city of mushrooms
filled to the brim with
grazing giraffes
and
death-dropping drag queens

i want to live in a fantasy

i want to be surrounded by
a fairy tale
coupled with
what our own world ought to be

loving
and caring
and inclusive
and free

i want to see women rule
in the forms of trolls,
centaurs and
supreme court justices

i want to feel power
over myself and my life
and i want to feel that

while dancing among fireflies

Gina Gil
Arlington, Virginia
Hour 24

Stardust

Stardust clouds
my mind when I contemplate
beginnings and endings. Both seem impossible
from where I stand,
in the middle.
Unable to imagine not existing
before or after this self I know now. Will I remain
and know who I am? Or forget everything
and dissolve back into stardust?

Ariel Westgard
Fort Myers, Florida
Hour 8

The Colors of My Life

I look around me and see the colors of my life.
The red cinnamon hot anger that flows through me when met with injustice.
The blue cold cascading water that flows over my body as I try to drown out my sadness.
The green zesty sour of limes as I feel jealousy spike through my blood.

These colors define me yet as I search, I realize I am missing some.

I am missing those happy colors –
The pink of sweet tarts as love fills my heart.

The yellow of a bright crayon that a toddler uses to color the sun.
The orange citrusy taste that fills my mouth as I laugh with my family and friends.

The colors of my life define me.

They create who I am and what I believe.
Yet a part of me always feels missing – like crayons have broken out from the box.

WREN
Wisconsin
Hour 4

Brokenly Inharmonious

Little by little
the space spreads;
it spreads between us
like wasted time,
robbing us of the many
more instances for our fingers to intertwine.

The tick-tock,
tick-tock of the metronome
forces the colors to change in the leaves.
Faster each time,
each time the tempo picks up.
The tempo picks up.

Where did all the spider webs come from?
We look back to the times
the music was lively,
lively and joyous.
Surely we could've kept
the melody from turning sour?

But sometimes,
sometimes the keys don't make the right sound
and we're left with an out of tune piano.

Our bodies give way
and like mannequins,
we stiffen.
We stiffen, letting the strings that bind us
become brokenly inharmonious.

Perhaps the piano was fine
and it was us who hit the wrong keys.

V.J.Calone
Lindenhurst, New York
Hour 2

The Time; it is Against Us

The time; it is against us.
How the hour is getting late. Wait!
Easy, Charlie... take your time and trust us.

Tempt fate and find your mate,
if you use what you have wisely.
Minutes, like dog-years blindly
erasing each hour off the clock.

"Invest your time wisely," they say.
Time flies when you are having fun this way.

"Into each life some rain must fall."
Surely, time is on my side."

Another hour, another year,
going in circles, have no fear.
Another trip around the pond,
in search of soulmate for a song.
Never mind the one-eyed toad,
stay in sight and off the road.
The mighty Mayfly takes to flight,

under the hosta and out of the light,
she appeared to his delight.

Blessing Omeiza Ojo
Abuja, Nigeria
Hour 22

In Which Every Sea Quavers with Tenderness

Ever had an uncle who would send you to buy him lunch
after gifting you some lashes on your buttocks?
He is not different from this home of terror
in which every tent owner quavers with fear
no matter how blue and calm the music playing beneath is.
We love this home still, even though the love she professed for us
is gone like a parrot who just got freedom from slavery.
And some of us,
once angelic to the bite of grief,
new to the singing of elegy, innocent of the fact
that the colour of our loved ones' blood poured
on the soil as libation to the hungry gods is the same as
that of barbarians that killed them,
harmonize in fear
and we are learning to be wild, to reflect our fears,
to defend our tomorrow, stationed at the mouth of the sea.
The memory bank says many of us have sunk into memory.
We, still alive, will not sink into this sea which is also a memory.
We write our grief and pain on our skin, our fears on the sky
for God to read it out to the angels in a guttural voice.
No matter how deep a poem is, it's not abysmal enough
to swallow our fear. At the reception, we are watching
the newlywed vibe to Buga*, a bang louder than gun's calls for attention.
We do not find the groom to say amen
to long life, amen to blissful home, amen to the taste of moon.

*A music that sends every gathering into frenzy in Nigeria

Mel Neet
Kansas City, Missouri
Hour 15

Nothingness

Gasps of organic matter stand frail sentry
in your doorways.
Willow wisps, meadow grass, chuffed wheat stalks, prairie blades
in every color known to Pantone
are referenced by your hosts.
All of your agents are thanked
and all of your rooms explored
no matter how similar.
These studies in skeletal flora
occupy molten pots heavy enough to be moveable only by Hercules
at pivot doors that reach the sky,
and we are hushed as we enter.
Rooms that will never be inhabited are set
as though for an episode of a late '90s dramatic series
in which every girl wore plum brown lipstick and
every boy ran his hands through his hair
to indicate concern.
Still, there's no lack of effect
in how unaffected every element in its undone-ness is.
For all its impenetrability,
– with its home theater, its bathrooms that outnumber its bedrooms, and its panic room –
the structure might as well be a dandelion.

Mandi Smith
Balch Springs, Dallas, Texas
Hour 8

A Mother's Love

I am the mother of four babies.
I wonder how it happened as I've never known a boy.
I hear my babies squealing, seeking sustenance and safety.
I see their empty eyes peering out from lifeless faces.
I want to feel their tiny heartbeats vibrate through my sore and swollen body as they suckle from my chest.
I am somehow broken; my babies all reject me.

I pretend there's not a problem.
I feel my heart shatter into pieces.
I touch their teeny tiny baby bodies, nudge them with my nose.
I worry I have failed them. I fear all hope is lost.
I cry out in despair, trying desperately to breathe life back into my babies.
I am now a mother of none.

I understand now I was never a mother, but my body believed I was.
I say these squishy, squealing squeak toys have always been my babies. *I dream* of fuzzy faces, of furry-footed foursomes that will one day call me MOTHER.
I try to listen closely as my master tells me we weren't all made to be mothers.
I hope she's majorly mistaken. Perhaps she's confused and crazy like I was.

I am a childless Chiweenie, desperate to be a doggy mama.

Chuks Oluigbo
Lagos, Nigeria
Hour 16

The World Grinds On

The world would grind on
when you lose your breath;
when, like a log, what's left
of you is heaved into the earth,
shovelfuls of dirt hitting
your resting box hewn from
any tree of the carpenter's fancy –
udara, melina, iroko, oak, mahogany –
who really cares?

Mourners would wipe dry eyes
and get on a feasting match –
God bless the dead
whose death
has brought us this bread.

Family would war to death
if you were of mega means;
some tear to shreds
even for meagre means.

A memorial a year if they cohere,
and, maybe, a reluctant visit to your
resting place, with paparazzi in tow,
just for the show.

Then, in time, everyone forgets
even your fondest jokes.
Now you're but a distant
thought, a faint memory,
for even those who remember
near their inevitable end.

It's not for want of love
or empathy; life burdens each
with not just a cross that even
the living forgets the living.

Interlude of the Heartbeats

"I have been waiting for you so long in my forever."

Atticus

Cynthia Hernandez
Bremerton, Washington
Hour 18

Sipping Joy

You showed up at my door
with a smile and a quick kiss.

I sipped joy all morning,
as I tasted your name.

Amrutha Nair
Barcelona, Spain
Hour 15

Cold

The cold creep up,
through the skin,
into the bones,
into the soul.
All I could do was
to think about you,
the warmth,
the heat.
Wonder what it did?
Was it warmth
or a sharp chill
right in the heart?
Our bodies were warm,
but the heart,
a bit too cold.
It kills me,
slowly,
and then,
all at once.

Gypsie-Ami Offenbacher-Ferris
Southport, North Carolina
Hour 5

The Date

The pavement hot beneath her sandaled feet,
walking briskly,
leather satchel swinging at her side.

Sitting in their favorite space
preparing the wine glass and
cheddar cheese, her favorite.

A lovely knitting gift,
a sunflower blanket beneath her,
allowed her dainty sandals to slide away.

Her satchel hanging on a nail
placed so long ago for just
that reason, on the old oak tree.

She could barely accommodate
her excitement and wonder,
being with him again this day.

Reverently, longingly, lovingly,
she pulled out her hardback novel,
opened it, and there he was.

Jana O'Dell
Charleston, West Virginia
Hour 18

Her

The way the orange and red shine upon her rose colored cheeks is
something I hope to never forget
The way the drips of rain gently flow down her skin is something I hope to
see a thousand times
The way the stars seem to all gather in her eyes as she looks at me is
something I hope I never become blind to
Yet here I am
Taking it all for granted
Knowing my whole galaxy lives within her
For some reason still choosing to close my eyes

Vijaya Gowrisankar
Mumbai, India
Hour 3

Distinct notes of togetherness

We are two violinists, with distinct personalities,
comfortable playing our own tunes,
creating and composing songs that depict our journey.

We are now a part of an orchestra, tasked with finding a rhythm,
to create songs together, to compose music that touches
our hearts, the hearts of our listeners.

How compelling is the music we play together, the notes
of high and low, in tune with life's challenges that we face
together and alone... the give and take, the showing up,

in the music, with the music, for the music... that resonate
with our core, that represent melody of when and where
life entwines... and separates, for each life - every song - is unique.

Elizabeth Durusau
Athens, Georgia
Hour 3

Dance with Me

Have this dance with me.
Run your fingers over the wood
and play a harmony.

Duets are forever dances,
even when we aren't moving
our feet to the rhythm.

And yet we are
as the notes fill the room
and we sway in time,

each of us shining
in our own way
with the music.

Stay with me
for this one dance
before the night is done.

Let me have
this moment with you
to keep forever in my heart.

DJ Delashmit
Covington, Tenenssee
Hour 6

Wither

I want to lay with you on a hand-stitched quilt on an open field full of sunflowers. My Darling Dear, like the flower, this too is our finest hour, and although we too will someday wither and fade, my Darling Dear, my love, no not today, no not today.

Simona Frosin
Galati, Romania
Hour 17

Painting rainbows

Will you receive me
under your umbrella
so that I do not get soaked?
It's easier and pleasant
to face this rain together!

And maybe we'll share ideas,
kisses and memories under
your generous umbrella.
Afterwards our heart
will paint rainbows.

Danielle Wong
Pierrefonds, Quebec, Canada
Hour 20

Ocean Love

Waves massage the beach
as quietly as they can
to carry breezes sweet
to the lovers on the land,
who sleep beneath the leaves
of the palms that did fan
the heat of passion's feet
away from the soft sand.

Kayla Aldan
Boardman, Ohio
Hour 6

I've Never Forgotten You

As trees lose their leaves,
and flowers lose their petals,
you left a piece of yourself with me
and I pressed that piece of you
into my heart.
I could keep you there,
the same way we take flowers and leaves
and press them between the pages of books
so we can have those reminders.

Amber L. Crabtree
Mesa, Arizona
Hour 15

In Your Eyes

Casually looking through photographs
I realiz your eyes remind me of
the most exquisite Labradorite.

They whisk me to a dimension
where my unattainable hopes and dreams
all come to fruition.

With you by my side my life comes alive.

Your love, the epitome of
romanticism in bloom,
tender hands dance through my Autumn-esque hair
during the nights we converse jubilantly.

Elegant, yet timid your heart tells me secrets
you've never divulged to another.

In the here and now, we facilitate our own suffering
as I wonder, do we have too much to give each other,
or not enough to matter?

Ivan Bekaren
Lagos, Nigeria
Hour 8

Show me all the stars

Silver speed in this bottle of unrest,

sweet deceit upon sensuous bare skin,
falling for this wild thing which brings us this wicked ease,
solemn confusion.

Veiled bliss, and enchanting power in secret places.

My senses linger long,
desire awakens strong,

and we're birthing escape bruises
before they mark our hearts...
birthing lust under this liquid scarlet glow.

No exit, only blinding ecstasy.
Silver speed in this bottle of unrest,

my senses linger long,
taking in shape, scent and pull of this bottle,
the sin of its instigating poise.

Now kill my innocence,
show me all the stars.

Brandee Charters
Dayton, Ohio
Hour 15

Burning...

I Want You Now
like I needed you then...

Fire races between us
when we are skin to skin.

So deep inside me
I yearn in pain...

Only you can fill me
make me whole again...

So far away
So close to my heart...

How can I live
with us so far apart?

Meghana Mandalappu
India
Hour 3

Ballerina

You smile across the table.
Your eyes locked with her dancing frame,
watching, observant, as she gets lost in the music.
She glides across the room,
each pirouette perfect,
each glissade on point.
She moves with grace,
a portrait of elegance.
She twirls in her pink tutu,
eyes closed as the music builds.
I see you fall deeper
as you observe her every move,
adoration sparkling in your eyes.
The last chord strikes,
her bright eyes cracking open,
meeting your piercing gaze.
She curtsies and smiles,
all eyes are on her
as she bows out,
leaving you to dream of her
under the city's stars.

Danielle Martin
Trinidad and Tobago
Hour 19

The City: Nightlife on the Avenue

I can't tell what hits my senses first
wafting musical notes or the
twinkling lights from sky and land

Maybe it's the
pungent rippling teasing smells
of fried chicken
of doubles
of hot wings
of mampie burgers
of gyros and Chinese too

Maybe it's the
sensation of skin brushing against skin
making way to the bar
or his gentle touch upon naked shoulders as we dance
to our song
for tonight every song is ours
the DJ is doing it right

Maybe it's the
drinks hitting my tongue playing with my thoughts
bringing laughter into the air
adding to the organismic vibe
that is this city by night

Jillian Calahan
Seattle, Washington
Hour 15

Eclipsing Beauty

How can you
look at your body,
soft and round,
and talk to it
the way that you do?
Even the earth gets
so jealous of the moon,
with all her curvatures,
that it will place itself
between her and the sun
just to eclipse its beauty.

Davita Joie
Boston, Massachusetts
Hour 2

Breathe

The woods are lovely, dark and deep,a perfect place for buried secrets.
Ghosts curl themselves around the fallen trunks and muddied stones,
the dank, decaying, sullen leaves.

I have been holding my breath
since I was fifteen
when the boy I loved biked to see me.

And here, decades later,
on the darkest evening of the year,
my breath returns with the force of a wailing banshee.
Under this canopy of strangled silence,
heart shattered in vengeful fury,
pieces drifting on the air like angry fireflies.

I have promises to keep,
but not to you.

Inspired by Robert Frost, "Stopping by Woods on a Snowy Evening"

Preeta Bhuyan
India
Hour 15

Never Ending Ache

the deep timbre of your voice
expending a nervous sensation
all through these sinewy veins
the holding of our gaze creating
a surge of blush to dimpled buccal
restless fingers wanting and waiting to entwine
and the magic of vacuum 'tween us
makes for a cloudy fog of a throb
always fearful of gesticulating, for it might
create a ripple, disturbing and distracting us
from the tense hypnotic air hanging dense
tearing it apart at the seam
reducing the magic to just a whim

so despite wanting to reduce the space between our palms
we don't
because who knows what may happen when the veiny hands
make its way over across every inch of this skin
will the cells awaken from their deep slumber?
raging like a hungry beast, devouring everything in its way?
or will it just be a reminder that
you always want what you can't have
or don't allow yourself to have
except for this ghost of a perpetual ache

Daun Wright
London, Ontario, Canada
Hour 15

Empty Soul

Lust snatches souls and minds, craters into an abyss of depravity.
The inability to pull back an impossible task as one plunges deeper and deeper

into a dark bottomless hole, helplessness prevails.
Escaping it unattainable, so one ventures deeper into a quagmire
of images and behaviors that taints the soul.

A profound desire to acquire wealth and possessions
and an unquenchable pull towards things left behind in departure, death!
Does it make sense then to live in the twirl of a whirlwind that makes you dizzy?
For as desire is satisfied after each new toy,
lust, a temporary feeling, bottoms out into nothingness,
leaving in its trail empty lives and broken people.

Lust snatches souls and leaves them mangled, like twisted metal from a car wreck!

Brett Dyer-Bolique and Valkyrie Kerry
Ireland
Hour 17

Carnivorous Carnival (Dyer-Bolique)

Hope plays the role contrite, L'art Cullinaire served on despair,
'You remember your place, my hold ever renewed!'
For what is flavour is loyalty, if yours is insipid impaired.

She basks on pleasantries, humouring my air,
Callously agreeable, contented, and shrewd.
Hope plays the role contrite, L'art Cullinaire served on despair.

As doe eyes adore, awaiting my approvals care,
'A pleasant idea,' a mock and impugn,
'For what is flavour is loyalty, if yours is insipid impaired'

'My canines are trained, versed in savageries prayer,
but fear not my heart, you they will not consume!'
Hope plays the role contrite, L'art Cullinaire served on despair.

She dances and connives, I see her in my vacant stare,
within my gaze, darkly dreaming visions accrue,
for what is flavour is loyalty, if yours is insipid impaired.

I have ensnared you once, for I am the fox to your hare,
'Tonight, we hunt, for flesh's atonement is due!'
For what is flavour is loyalty, if yours is insipid impaired,
hope plays the role contrite, L'art Cullinaire served on despair.

L'Art Cullinaire (Valkyrie)

Crimson candles glow, meaty cutlets served,
romanticised date, I remember you,
first desirous date, feigning fear reserved.

'What is this sweet meat?' More than I deserved,
passions rekindled, guilt for doubting you,
crimson candles glow, meaty cutlets served.

Evil smirk spreads, 'Your arm I had preserved!'
Guilt abates, once again your colours true,
first desirous date, feigning fear reserved.

'Raising two wolves, their hunger I observed,
and fed them meat cutlets as one must do,'
Crimson candles glow, meaty cutlets served.

I hide my horror, submission subserved,
taking each mouthful, I carefully chew,
first desirous date, feigning fear reserved.

My resolve steady, plan in place deserved,
'Werewolves made great horror beasts too, that slew!'
Crimson candles glow, meaty cutlets served,
first desirous date, feigning fear reserved.

Morsels of Memories

"Each time I think I've created time for myself, along comes a throwback to disrupt my private space."

Wole Soyinka

David Bruce Patterson
Bracebridge, Ontario, Canada
Hour 15

A Tribute to Emily Dickinson "Berries"

I taste a concoction,
an investment of time
sublime. In the elegance of the heritage crystal
of berries so rich and royal;
such potency!

The family room
takes on an air of inebriation,
like the carpet is dewed
with aged cherry;
a merry playful mist ensues.

There are words of nectar,
wine and fortification,
going to fine Inns,
to carry on this rousing.
Shall there be but more?

This, the soup of hope,
in nature's bowl.
Our souls the spoon of courage
and wonder,
rimmed with idle curiosity.

Sweet and sour,
the pain of what draws me
and the joy of dawning retreat;
the victory of my shelter,
whether wood or a broken heart.

The little miracles
in frantic flight;
the sight of buzzing Bees
in their visitation
of fragrant passing,
tasting
a part of me.

Margarette Wahl
Long Island, New York
Hour 12

Sounds of His Chuckle

In memory of Francis Maiorino

His son recites a script as he records
the hilarity behind his phone,
full of life and merriment.
A time where he seems
happy,
glee in belly giggles
recorded on his IG.
This derision, such an
illusion, now
four months since he passed
away.
A jollity worth
remembering,
I watch it over and over,
never growing tired of his
snigger.
His jest reminds me of his
days
in Junior High; caught him
in trouble
snickering still.

Shirley Durr
Minneapolis, Minnesota
Hour 22

Monarch Butterfly a Wing

Did the title tap memories of feelings so right
they moved your heart higher than a soaring kite?
Did you imagine yourself in a meadow so bright
the colors would bind you in endless delight
while wandering waterbirds dance and excite
You? Did you assume serenity would land your sight
on a monarch butterfly caught in mid-flight
while skimming and skipping over lakes so lightly,
ephemeral motion, in stillness made mightily
calm, profoundly full of meaning and insight?

You suppose wrong; the title's not a typo.

Stepping out of the church's front door —
in a fog of solemn sorrow and ire
after a troubling memorial service
for a troubled sister who had left me
hurt, angry, too soon, and unresolved —
I glimpsed a butterfly wing on the sidewalk
just before my next step would crush it.

I froze in thought, "Oh, Butterfly!
Where have you gone?"
And remembered my much-admired beloved sister.
I spoke to the missing piece,
"Are you still flying on one wing?"
And remembered my enigmatic, wounded sister.

My mind's eye created instant poetry:
"Did some jealous god capture you
to rip your wing
from your frail body
then spirited you away
and left you forsaken
far from your wing
to seal the separation?"
And remembered my fiercely gifted sister.

(Oh, my sister!
No one ever – before or since –
so close to me
so far apart.)

All in a fleeting moment
I stooped to gather up the wing —
ignoring voices speaking comfort,
hugs seeking to console me
with joys in their memory of her.

Rejecting those useless cares,
while remembering them kindly.
I tucked their memories and my wing
between two pages of eulogy
and took them home with me
to wash myself in all the unshed tears
drowning me in despair.
They're still here – the memories and the wing —
on the wooden box that holds her ashes.

On that otherwise empty bookshelf,
the dust covers happy memories
and she (oh, butterfly!) looks so forlorn;
in my dreams she's flying.
In her life I dreamed I could make her whole again;
she would not land long enough to let me.

When I saw a craft vendor tossing away
a wooden dragonfly with one wing missing,
I offered to buy it; we bargained for two:
one whole and the other I wanted.

I keep the dragonflies on the ashes box,
placing the butterfly wing
where the dragonfly's is missing.

The dragonflies stay still.
But every now and then
the wing
moves —
Is it trying to fly? —

Once the wing fell and was lost
to me.

I recovered it
while dusting behind the box.

Sometimes I forget the whole one;
even when it's there, I don't see.
I allow the sight of the wounded one —
and the wing — to haunt me,
knowing the butterfly will never be whole
but hoping to one day reach
Solace and Resolution.

Yet,
maybe I began this wrong.
Perhaps, after all,
this will be
about finding serenity
while watching a butterfly, a wing.

Thryaksha
Chennai, India
Hour 23

Lady Midnight

An unequal world served as her beckoning.
It was an everyday battle for her every right.
She vowed to be a queen in the tyranny of the king,
looking for passages and tunnels for hiding.
She moved silently in the cover of the night.
The unequal world served as her beckoning.
She knew when to attack and when to take a swing,
to come back and live for another fight.
She'd be a queen in the tyranny of the king.
She spent her time training and waiting, biding,
taught herself lessons from a helpful knight.
The unequal world would surely cause her beckoning.
She paid her dues and hellfire she did bring,
the guards and the king froze at the sight.
She knew she'd be a queen in the tyranny of the king.
She christened herself Queen at her own crowning,
with the blessing of the universe under the starlight.
In an unequal world, which served as her beckoning,
She was the queen in a tyranny of the king.

Cindy P. Whitaker
Durango, Colorado
Hour 5

The Sunflowers Bobbed

He came home for the funeral; things looked much as when he had visited at Christmas.
Working overseas for a homeland security company had kept him away a lot after 911.

Hymns, sandwiches, hugs and tears during the old-fashioned church service seemed surreal.
Family, friends, and friends like family gathered and rallied. She was well loved by all.

They talked every Sunday; facetiming had held no appeal although they had attempted it once or twice.
He couldn't believe his dear grandmother had passed away so suddenly. What a shock! A terrible shock!

He sat down and thought about growing up in this house; her love and care surrounded him.
Looking for keepsakes wasn't why he lingered; he had simply come to say goodbye. And thank you.

A ten-year-old best seller, a large print hardback, lie open on the threadbare lounger.
The knitting basket had tipped over and colorful balls of yard had spilled out onto the floor.

Just outside the kitchen window, a garden of sunflowers bobbed, twisted and strained toward the sun.
The grand old oak stood as still as a sentry at the corner of the yard, nestled by crumbling pavement.

The nail holding down a corner of the carpet was rough and bent, collecting extra dirt in the space.
An empty wineglass sat unattended on the back patio; a cloth napkin had blown under the chair.

A recipe for Gma's famous au gratin potatoes hung front and center on the frig; held snug by a huge "Got Beef?" Magnet.
She had made that casserole for every church potluck; Tillamook cheese was her secret ingredient.

A stack of all the postcards and letters he had written her were buried in the bottom of her worn leather satchel.
He knew he'd find them there, along with a few smooth rocks from the Oregon coast and a tiny stuffed owl.

He walked around one more time; he bent down to grab her "helpers" and sat them next to the book.
He decided there was no need to clean up or pick up; memories like his could not be boxed up.

Jill Halasz
Texas City, Texas
Hour 1

The Seashell

I took my baby to the beach;
I walked her to the water,
a million seashells in our reach.
A day for Mom and daughter;
a moment that had harkened back
to days spent in my youth.
My Dad and I had quite the knack
of finding hope and truth.

How does one find truth and hope?
Within a simple shell,
each one has the means to cope,
amid each ocean swell;
a story that one can all but guess,
that brought it here this day.
But one I stand here to profess
is profound in its way.

Up against the ocean's odds,
the shell has bounced along.
its fate left only to the gods
amid the currents' strong.
Yet here it stands within our hands,
so perfect and pristine,
upon arrival to the lands
on water, crystalline.

I took my daughter to the beach,
a day of summer fun.
Fond memories within my reach,
beneath the summer sun;
for not just searching for the shells
but stopping to think too.
Despite the many ocean swells,
the seashell made it through.

The day became a blessing
for my daughter to recall.
The shell is but a lesson
of survival for us all.
A symbol of the will and might,
we all hold deep inside,
that carries us past every plight,
to reach our shores in stride.

Ayah April Soliman
Salt Spring Island, British Columbia, Canada
Hour 22

Tenderness

I wonder who you could have been?
That part of you trapped within.
That little one; if only, you were treasured
with "I believe in you's" and love assured.

I wonder what you could have been?
If resentment didn't cage you in,
sunk to "black sheep" of the family,
always having to question your sanity.

I wonder where you could have been?
If not that hostile place you were in.
A disconnected, inconsistent, trap;
any wrong move and they would snap.

I wonder how you could have been?
If the mother you knew took you in-
to the tenderness she threw away,
but you always had to somehow pay.

Cut down to a shell of self-sabotage.
Growing up disorientated in camouflage.
Anguished and torn over the scorn,
sewn within your own flesh and blood.

Now it's on you to bury them in mud.
You got lost trying to "raise" them up,
with brokenness and an empty cup.

Searching for love and belonging,
the motherless ache always dawning.
One by one lovers filled your cup.
One by one they gave you up.
Threw you out of their lives like junk.
Packed up in a dim, pitiful trunk.

I wonder...
If life didn't echo what was dragged behind?
Trying to escape the demons of your mind.

If you could just let go and look high above,
past the pseudo storms of filtered fake love,
and reach for Him, a love so endless and sincere,
slamming all the doors to pain, trauma and fear.

Pacella Chukwuma Eke
Abuja, Nigeria
Hour 2

History of Summer and Winter

Inspired by Stopping by the woods on a snowy evening

The woods are lovely, dark & deep.
Robert Frost

i. Lovely/Summer
My parents built a nest in the woods.
I had plucked a star from
a boy's lips.
Brother drew color on his chin
and we buried our hearts inside
a tree's skin.

Ii. Dark/Winter
Ice stole Paa away from me.
Mother lost her voice to the
snowflakes of penury.
Brother got raped by a rainbow
and my identity scurried away
 as we walked home.

Iii. Summer/Deep
Brother would be going for a tour
to the sky's edge, with his lover.
A boy is locking my heart in a chest
made of his own flesh
and Mother is learning to speak
for the first time, after winter.

Presley Tieman
Florida
Hour 7

Ordinary

One lifetime is not enough to love you
when I couldn't wait to say "I do."
Doing laundry and taxes are mundane,
but no day spent with you is spent in vain.

Loving you comes with ease
so in the next life will you find me, please.
They say when you take care of things,
they last. And I can't wait to see what forever brings.

David L. Wilson
Wailuku, Hawaii
Hour 7

Too Many Syllables for a Haiku

Before I met my wife
I was as lonely as an empty bookshelf
denying the existence of books

Lakita Gayden
Chicago, Illinois
Hour 16

Limerick

There once was an infant from Illinois
who ate or dismantled her toys

Her teeth tore through tires
Her hands gripped like steel pliers

Unscrewing chair nuts and bolts brought her joy

Mary Pecaut
Panama City, Panama
Hour 17

Apartment Living

My disgruntled neighbor

lives

under

    the

        stairs

The noise complaining basilisk

kills with a single glare.

Or maybe

    he's a sea

serpent

    eager

for war

    a scaly-skin

kraken

    of maritime lore.

I want to be a friendly tenant

and figure we should meet.

So, I bring him a plate of papayas

not knowing what a monster might eat.

Zeenat Razzak Shaikh
Pune City, Maharashtra, India
Hour 15

In her Eyes

Mummy sits still
surrounded by us three
She is the perfect narrator
Her small smile widens and spreads across her face
as she slowly unravels her childhood tales
How she'd pluck guavas with her siblings
Times when they stole money
swimming in rivers
eating tamarind
Her eyes gleam with joy
the perfect small rounds enlarged
Her face contracts in a way
that surges pleasure in my heart at a high rate
Long walks for water
Mishaps, accidents and fights
She tells us how my grandpa chose her as my father's bride
We have heard her tales multiple times
Yet, every time we listen eagerly with no interruptions.
In her eyes we see
who she was before being our mother
A charmer
A beauty
Someone who'd live their lives to fullest
Now she is just a responsible mother.

Divya Venkateswaran
India
Hour 6

One of Many

I sometimes wonder
If you could ever conclude
The depth of my emotions
The rug you pulled underneath me
I showed you all the love I could give
It's worrying that you do not understand love
The way I do, "I Love You" doesn't resound
I have felt you near me, even when you were far
You say I anchor your fleeting thoughts
Calm the storm inside you
That your soul recognizes mine
But you still don't understand my love
My love for you that ever was
I am tired of showing my love to you
I now lie silent at peace
The same peace, which you said you see in me.
Yours lovingly
The Poet

Locomotive Locales

"The greatest secrets are always hidden in the most unlikely places."

Roald Dahl

Margo Wilson
Dunnellon, Florida
Hour 19

Dunnellon

Dunnellon is a place I couldn't have imagined as my dwelling when I lived in L.A.
Five stoplights. One Walmart. No bookstore. No Starbucks.

I moved here, sight unseen, for various reasons we don't have to go into.

This is not supposed to be a nature poem, but Dunnellon is a nature city, more so than Thunder Bay, home of mountainous snowbanks blown off Lake Superior,
or Monessen, atop the green rolling hills of Pennsylvania.

Deer, ibis, armadillos, and wild boars strut near my door.

Dunnellon strides the Rainbow and Withlacoochee Rivers. The Rainbow is a well of spring water, whose bottom undulates through looking-glass ripples.

The Withlacoochee is a different matter. Alligators sun on its banks and the weeds grow deep.

Snowbirds make their homes here much of the year.
But in the deepest part of the summer,
when the sun bears down and the humidity clings,
Dunnellon is my place, humming and thrumming,
growing and raining,

a Garden of Eden in my backyard.

Anjum Wasim Dar
Islamabad, Pakistan
Hour 12

Ode to a Nigerian Piece of Art

O thou unbeaten, unsounded circular percussion,
I admire thee!
Placed elegantly in bride-like silence
in historical African time,
your smooth silky top, classically stitched
with legendary leather, patterns criss-crossed,
holds to secure the haunting beats-

What romantic tales bang out,
what messages sweet,
what calls for secret help,
what melodies or saddened grieves!

O thou classic beat,
flanked by sturdy woven seats
and a royal blue vase to complete
the ancient kingdom's high seat.

O thou African beauty,
I admire thee!
Thou hast thy music and grace.
Soon the silence will break,
thou shalt remain forever,
beating out love and eternal peace.

Sabinah Adewole
United Kingdom
Hour 15

Kusadasi

The way to Samos,
the green palm trees
stood tall.
The blue sky,
houses built on rocks,
picturesque view.
The castle in the corner,
busy with character,
buzzing with life.
Love of family,
the shops in the marina.
The coffee shop,
tourists arriving,
vacationers in diversity.
The beauty of leaving,
the harbour front,
the waiting coaches.
Kebab corner shops,
Turkish tea on offer.
The cruise in waiting,
the business in the city,
such a vibrant town.
Kusadasi inscribed on
the mountain top.
The friendly locals,
one shop on to another.
Terzi means tailor.
The Beauty of life.

Jarrod Fouts
Griffin, Georgia
Hour 22

After Texas

It started with solar panel smashings
fields were littered with the black spaceware
twinkling in shards in the sun

next, they took down the turbines
they were felled during maintenance
Some unaware workers were seen on top
embracing before jumping together

from there, the hydroelectric dam
hole blown in wall by homemade device
thousands of gallons crashed through
drowning what must have been thought of
as an acceptable cost

finally, the reactors melted down
and the demon elephant's foot
that amassed itself in Chernobyl
paled in comparison
to a new creature of uranium
we can't even name

soon the smog and choke returned
and every anti-green warrior
worshipped again at the oil rigs and
returned to the mines deep below
to be crushed in collapses and have their lungs blackened
dying, yet feeling so free
pulling us with them into an Earth on fire.

Aleta D. Nolan
Alva, Oklahoma
Hour 6

The Sneaky Librarian

There is a librarian
down on 7th street
in a tiny town library
with gigantic feet.

I've seen them you know,
those gigantic feet
in the tiny town library
down on 7th street.

I peeked through the window
in the library door.
She took her shoes off
and danced over the floor.

I laughed and I giggled
to watch those feet
in the tiny town library
down on 7th street.

The librarian looked up
I knew it was time
to run for the hills
or the next dance was mine.

Betty Jean Steinshouer
Florida
Hour 9

Spam

I laugh uproariously at the amusing song
by Cheryl Wheeler, about the cruise ship
that got stranded out at sea, and
all they had to eat for a couple of weeks
was pop tarts and spam, airlifted from the mainland.
No one, from the most accomplished chef in a French café
to the short-order cook in the greasy spoon, could make
a fine meal out of those ingredients. Not enough bechamel
sauce in all of France to dress up that awful can-shaped
substance. Yet when we were young, eleven kids starving on a
cold-water farm in the Ozarks, spam was the great luxury.
We all waited, stair steps from four to twenty, eager for our slice,
browned around the edges from the skillet, and delicious.

Dexta Jean Rodriguez
Ozark Mountains, Russellville, Arkansas
Hour 17

Subbing in America through Haiku

The first day they learn
conveyor belt of children
red apple for lunch

Bollimuntha Venkata Ramana Rao
Telangana state, India
Hour 19

City Lights

When the play came to an end
at last the lights switch off
The curtain closes on the podium

Tonight, the city under the firmament
folded as a black blanket
Congregation of the stars in the sky
Wind chants melody tunes a lullaby
The streets lights guard like a hawk

In palm tree-like houses
They embrace dreams
in their azure dreams
It that black dark night
The silence is also frightening.

This city for me now
peeps it as a blackboard
the pedagogue erased characters
for next day class

Tobe T Tomlinson
Essex, Vermont
Hour 10

Understand

Metal door creaks open rusty mailbox
Blaze red flame decals flaking off warns
Do not step in front of passing cars

Though the library waits paces away
I remain eager to grab that packaged
book inside to read after dark

Only banned books this summer will
teach me how to know and feel a world
remote from my country graveled drive

Understand how it is for others beyond
this clapboard farmhouse in need of paint
I learn with sincere and humble intention

A Dip into Metaphors

"That the moon is the eye of the night."

Han Kang

Bhasha Dwivedi
Lucknow, India
Hour 6

The Dragon on the Branch

High upon the tallest tree,
on the wooden branches,
perched a dragon,
looking out into the sea.

Its wings all curled up
(I wonder how big they must be);
its scales gleaming in the rays
of setting sun scattered through the sea.

And I looked and looked at it some more,
while waiting – for something to happen,
for it to move or lean or stretch or…
Anything really!

But still it sat with wooden eyes,
on the high branch of the tree;
just, simply, plainly
looking over the sea when–

The ringing classroom bell brought me back to real life,
where maths problems were the reality,
and dragons on branches existed only in crevices of bored minds,
imagination fueled by lack of fantasy.

With a last look outside the window,
I sighed as I moved on to another story,
entirely missing the dragon on the branch,
finally unfurling its wings and flying towards the sea.

J R Turek
East Meadow, New York
Hour 23

DogSpeak: Employment Application

Name
The Dog

Skills
Retriever
fetch and fill with slobber,
shred into crosscut pieces

Landscaper
unearth anything that makes noise
or smells bad; digger, unplanter, uprooter

Demolition Expert
any material, no job too big or small;
no clean-up included

Bounty Hunter
animal, vegetable, mineral
anything, anywhere, delivered dead
      unless otherwise specified

Refrigerator Janitor
clean and clean-out but no kale,
broccoli, spinach, nothing green

Greeter
kisses and free hugs
non-discriminatory, though cats are iffy

Education
still learning from every fire hydrant,
tree, and bush in my neighborhood
no degree; mutt

Race (optional)
often, especially down the stairs

Age (optional)
in dog years or human years?

Any Allergies We Should Know About
cats

Available Shifts
between naps and meals

Salary Desired
bones, kibble, treats, toys
gas money for my humans

When Can You Start
after lunch but I have to be home for dinner
I can't stay out after dark

References
Chance, Pebbles, Buster, Opie, Snickers,
Munchkin, Gumball, the man who runs
the dog park, my humans

Preferred Contact Method
whistle

Angie Mountain
Ambler, Pennsylvania
Hour 5

Chipmunk

I peered outside the bathroom window
early this morning, while the
house was still asleep,
looking for the chipmunk
whose acquaintance I first made
upon our late afternoon arrival
just the day before.

A little long and skinny, I thought,
for a chipmunk, but almond brown
with black and white stripes clearly
racing down his narrow back.
I expected to see him, somehow,
though I have no knowledge
of his usual comings and goings.

The mud-and-grass patched ground
lay still and empty, devoid of
chipmunks or, indeed, any living creature.
And I was strangely disappointed,
as though the chipmunk had become,
in actuality, my friend, and had
thoughtlessly ignored my invitation.

Cheryl Mitchell
Inglewood, Ontario, Canada
Hour 24

May Queen

the forest floor is triumphant;
a platoon of purple petals, skyward
and trumpeting their own arrival

exuberant mosses explode like champagne foam,
to make a home on rocks and trunks and crevices
amongst the riotous yellow cheer of bladderwort

winged creatures dance in their lady slippers
to an orchestra of bird song
and through a buffet of bitter lettuce, wild mint and thistle

the whistle of wind moving the grasses to sway and swoon
in a collective appreciation of this springtime afternoon
the diva fern with her maiden hair watches from a distance,
her resistance more than futile in this constant forest flurry

the scurrying of squirrels, their tails bouncing through the brush
a busy rush, a scamper, to gather up some nuts
a spider puts up streamers and calls the flies to play
it is a party of plenitudes for the reigning Queen of May

Joy Miller
Elkton, Oregon
Hour 24

Stardust is Made of Cheese

"Stardust is made of cheese
asleep in its own shoes,"
my mind repeats,
hoping for a little of each.

Sleep first. That glorious time
when movies and music play;
and I, the star, am the hero
hoping for a resolution.

Then cheese, and showers,
and shoes, and tea;
water with lime and mint
as I play examining stardust.

Carol Prost
Maynard, Massachusetts
Hour 17

Strawberry Moon

rising crimson orb of night, large against the starry sky
full of herself and unafraid to bedazzle.
the sweet red flesh of passion bends the stem
to the soft June ground, where
field mice and voles sink their
pointy teeth into each berry, then
quickly move on to the next.
ruby lips dripping summer's feast
in the magic of moonlight.

Half Marathon Poems

Two Years On (And Still Counting)

"At the end of the day, we can endure much more than we think we can."

Frida Kahlo

Vidhi Ashar
Bangalore, India
Hour 15

winter solstice

winter solstice
the familiar warmth of
i s o l a t i o n

Jan Rog
Kansas City, Missouri
Hour 12

Summer Gatherings of Old and Anew

While camping we'd scatter
to capture golden fireflies
dancing in an ebony sky
or
yellow butterflies gracing
a blue heaven
before we'd circle 'round, tip heads together,
open jars, and release them to freedom.

Hazy summer days when concrete
sizzled and steamed
we'd splash in opened hydrants
or
lay blankets side by side on welcoming
green grass while music played in parks.
Alongside our neighbors, we'd dance or sing
finding coolness in spontaneous community.

Bustling, bumping, jolting, and jostling
came with all our summer rituals,
like noisy, daily bus rides delivering us to
ball games with hot dogs, art classes in galleries,
mischievous adventures along crowded streets;
we all joined and journeyed together.

Whether a child or the sage adult I grew to be,
I looked forward to summer gatherings.
Suddenly older and cautious,
I cherish calm rituals with a few loved ones
as we slowly emerge from behind our masks.
I grow content with my smaller, deeper world,
shyly connecting with others as I see them with softer eyes.
Still beautiful, yet now wistful, summer gatherings have transformed me.

Kristin Cleage
Atlanta, Georgia
Hour 12

Plague Year Three or is it Four?

Will we ever gather again like
we used to? Maybe the younger ones
will. They already do. Us old folks,
not ready to die yet, we'll gather in
dibs and dabs. A child and their children
here, another child there. A granddaughter,
a grandson. A visit masked. A visit after
testing.

Thanksgiving eve was the last big
gathering for us. After that, the covid
meandered through the family, up one side and
down the other, hitting some twice.

The novelty of zooming long
gone. Plague without end. Thankful
we're all still on
this side.

Anwar Suleman
Johannesburg, South Africa
Hour 12

GATHERINGS POST PANDEMIC

Lockdowns and restrictions rescinded,
gatherings are now permitted,
as the pandemic marches towards a decline,
with family and friends, we can now recline.

But wait!!!!
My mind is in anguished debate!
Am I ready for a forward surge?
From my cocoon to emerge?
To shed my safety covering?
Like a social butterfly, to now be fluttering?

I WILL venture out, once again.
But before the worldly gatherings conspire to seduce,
at least let me enjoy and retain,
one more day to be a recluse!

Cristy Watson
Calgary, Alberta, Canada
Hour 12

a gathering of poets

around a drum
the room filled with inspiration
we gather to share our words. the long haul
of covid slowly behind us, some still donning masks,
we hear the rustle of paper, the shuffle of feet,
and a chorus of snapping fingers when
the lines are done. nodding heads and contemplative
murmurs at the turn of a phrase, the twist
of a rhyme, and the toe-tapping beat of the metre. how
we missed this sustenance over the past two years—
the heartbeat of metaphors, the pop-off-the page
imagery that brings us right into the poet's mind,
and how a simple word can pull a broken world
back together.

Undone (Roe Vs. Wade and the Fallout)

"The strongest principle of growth lies in the human choice."

Mary Ann Evans, who published under the name, George Eliot.

Tricia L. Somers
Los Angeles, California
Hour 9

Woman With A Top Hat

Woman with a top hat
had to dress up like a man.

Opinions of misogynists
switched up to laws

with no argument, debate
or basic common decency.

Cut her hair.
Tweaked her name.

Said she would be damned
if she was gonna be robbed.

She wasn't gonna give back
her share of the empire

females helped to build.
So instead, she calls herself Rob.

She gets to keep her autonomy.
Not to mention her humanity.

Erin Lorandos
Phoenix, Arizona
Hour 10

and Raven was silent

on the day the world turned dark
fifty years became dust under our feet
again, we marched for freedoms we had yesterday,
and tears flowed, through smoke and anger

she, black beauty, keen eye –
looked the other way
when reason lost out to returns
and the only color the men saw, was power

the spirits of our mothers no longer
speak to us, we are now the lost souls

and Raven is silent

Andrew Shaughnessy
Toronto, Ontario
Hour 1

The Day After the Bomb Went Off

The morning, silent and still,
betrayed the overwhelming
news that a bomb
had gone off,
leaving those who planned

for this ominous event for
years, as well as those
caught after years
of complacency
and self-denial, to marvel
at its occurrence and to plot

the contours of the shadow
that the plume from this
destruction
would have
on future years and lives.

As a dinosaur must have thought
while viewing the meteor
hurtling to
an innocent earth:
'How the hell will this work out?'

How the hell indeed.

Susan Hannon
Palm Desert, California
Hour 4

Wanted and Not Wanted

Roe vs Wade was overturned today.

I walked into the break room and found
my coffee pot gone.

Elsewhere a teenage girl found she'll have to carry
her father's baby to term.

I walked next door to the coffee shop,
snuck out of work unseen but
their coffee was weak and I needed caffeine.

She went to a neighboring state
and found out she was too far along
but at least she won't be accused of murder
when she returns home.

A year ago this time,
mass graves were found
of indigenous children killed a hundred years ago
at old residential schools.
They were stolen from their parents.
These children were wanted and they were not wanted.

Three years ago in Perris California
thirteen children were found
imprisoned by their parents
tortured in their house of horrors
allowed to eat once a day,
shower once a year;
kept chained to their beds.
These children were wanted and they were not wanted.

Roe vs. Wade was overturned today.

The coffee pot was gone from my break room.

And a girl realized her only hope to not bear her father's child
had been taken away.

Laura Daniels
Mt Arlington, New Jersey
Hour 4

Change? What Change?

A hundred years ago in 1922
women's suffrage was beginning.
Weapons were pistols, rifles, and Tommy guns;
the 19th amendment passed, but women wanted more.
Tommy guns were reserved for gangsters and movies.

Now in 2022
abortion is ruled illegal, dissolving a fifty-year right.
Open carry of a firearm is the law of the land;
states can decide what a woman can do with her body.
Something as simple as a zip code can determine rights and safety.

A hundred years from now in 2122
Will we still be denying women human rights or worse?
Will we still subject women to backstreet abortions or worse?
Will we still be allowing open carry of assault rifles or worse?
Will innocent children and bystanders still be getting gunned down or worse?

Ashay Mathieu
Los Angeles, California
Hour 2

Darkest Night

The darkest evening of the year was the night six people stole women's constitutional rights.
The darkest evening of the year was the silence in Uvalde, Texas where the souls of twenty-one people left this earth because of gun violence.
The deepness of these tragedies only reflect the heart of our American humanity.
Who is listening to the outcries of the families of eleven black souls gunned down in a NYC town?
Now that is the "the darkest evening of the year", Robert Frost!
Robert did not know this day would come, perhaps with the hope of our divine one's
intervention,
tomorrow night will be better? I will pray, wait and see.

Leila Tualla
Spring, Texas
Hour 1

and the women cried

the world is on fire
and i can feel the immense heat;
can smell the flesh of trees burning,

hear the agony and cries of the earth.

i want and need the deluge to come
and cleanse us and give life back to these
parched lands. but the water does not come;
instead tears spring from within.

and all the women cried in fury –
their tears giving hope,
life,
soothing the heat of their aching heart.

the world is on fire
but the women are not the ones burning.

Kathleen Tighe
Sand Point, Michigan
Hour 3

Shades

I saw amber waves of grain
in a dream it must have been
for they stretched for miles, so far,
coast to coast, it seemed,
and overtook all means to stop them.
Fruitful they were, multiplying by the thousands,
millions even,
standing tall,
waving in the breeze,
effortlessly bending,
and thus,
unbreakable.
And then, as one – a mirage? But no –
the amber shifted, not gradually,
as when the season changes
from summer to fall,
but all at once
as when a sudden summer storm breaks –
electrical currents wreaking havoc –
and those amber fields of grain,
burst brilliantly into pink!
Proud and vibrant and
unabashedly female –
the boldness of azaleas,
magenta and fuchsia,
and the blush of peonies
and tulips' petals;
subtle hues of coral and dusty rosewood,
terracotta, and salmon;
the pastels of bubble gum and babies' cheeks,
of cotton candy,
and flamingos.
Onward they marched,
fierce fields of persistence,
until all was afire in pink,
a rosy glow enveloping the nation,
a spark growing into a blaze
of fury.

Natalie Croney
Bowling Green, Kentucky
Hour 2

Hollowed Spaces

"Because if you weren't an Aunt or a Martha, said Aunt Vidala, what earthly use were you if you didn't have a baby?" (Margaret Atwood in The Testaments: The Sequel to The Handmaid's Tale)

The word womb.
The speakers of Old English used the word for belly, bowels, heart, uterus.
Isn't it amazing that it uses all forms of the word carry?
It holds like a bowl
like the barrel of a gun
like Hermes.

My last ultrasound was quiet, hollow, void
as it should have been.
The only thing that I would have born
would have been parasitic and violent,

But the quiet still gutted me.
There is something solemn about an empty womb.
To see it hallowed like a sanctuary, or
hollowed out like a cave
An echoing image of what could be – for better or worse–
another life.

Sobriety occurs when I have a sneaking suspicion
That the gods aborted all of my babies for me.
Do I say thank you or scream until there's a cave-in?

Colleen Schwartz
Bellingham, Washington
Hour 8

Riptide

Like a river after a storm
strong, unseen currents

leave me gasping for breath
for safety
for some glimmer of hope

The Decision feels like a riptide
searing the fabric of my assuredness

and my solidity feels tenuous
along this shoreline

my strong banks may shudder
like a river after a storm

The Decision feels like a riptide
carrying survivors
far away from shelter

farther still – from the breasts
of our grandmothers and aunties

Jo Eckler
Austin, Texas
Hour 3

The Scales

They say it's my Libra sun
I can't escape my craving for balance
Even now I crush gingery Biscoff cookies into the chilly vanilla ice cream
Yearning to force fairness
into a highly unjust time
Crumbling (for a moment) when I can't find warmth in the cold.

Articulations (About our world... One another... Ourselves)

"Hope is the thing with feathers that perches in the soul..."

Emily Dickinson

Shloka Shankar
Bangalore, India
Hour 14

summer skies

a clutch of birds
        alters the composition
                summer skies

Mahima Giri
Houston, Texas
Hour 5

dormant chills of night
kiss nocturnal auroras-
glimmering fireflies

Juvairiya Sulthana
Barakath Nagar
Hour Unknown

The Strawberry Moon

In the dark night, the strawberry moonlight shines on me, while I stand on the edge of the mountain.

The night is beautiful—with the sweet smells, the crisp air, and everything around me.

The strawberry moonlight illuminates a comet and shooting
star as they cross paths over the earth.

The stars are like small diamonds—
the sky, a mix of purple and blue.

My every pain vanished tonight.
Now to sleep—my dreams filled with happiness.

I feel like I am standing in heaven;
a night I will never forget, for all my life.

Aferdita Blaka
Tirana, Albania
Hour Unknown

Autumn, Coming!

Autumn has come,
so pretty with her graces,
dressed in many colors,
with wet mantle, worn!

The sun warms lightly,
touches the leaves slowly,
wind flows with whispers,
one by one, taking them down.

Away heavy branches!
Almost touching the ground,
their arms hanging,
like gathering babies.

Wet is this season,
watching the steps done,
thunder and sparks come,
then the sun scatters its rays.

This is how the seasons flow,
beginning with summer's blooming buds,
warm, summer keeps them,
while autumn gathers fruit
for winter, with its white beard!

Eh, how am I,
autumn, it seems to me,
in my lap, swaddling the babies,
yellowed leaves, with gray on my head!

I rejoice and enjoy,
with the dancing of colors,
I take care of the seedlings,
as before, when in my first season!

Nancy Ann Smith
Amherst, Ohio
Hour 1

Long Awaited

Waiting for days,
everyone waits,
patiently
or impatiently
everything is waiting –
farmers, gardeners, workers
crops, lawns, gardens.

Then –
I shiver, just a bit.
Temperature drops two degrees.
The sun has nodded off;
the clouds no longer white puff balls.
Something is different . . .

Walking from the garden to the house
there has been nothing to harvest,
even weeds are wilting.
Hot afternoons – how many in a row?
The first drops are too strange to recognize.
My mind is on a pasta salad, without
peppers, tomatoes, green onions.

OH!
I finally feel the distinct wet spot
dotting my bare arm.
Unsure, unfamiliar,
I have to double check.
Is that brown ground truly speckled?
YES!   Thank you, Lord!

Jan Meyer
Cedar Park, Texas
Hour Unknown

Flora Music

Confident rose gold tree	surveying the field around her.

Cocking her head gently to the side	she waves to the fuchsia
flowers   honoring

her with their profusion	of deep pink passion.

She's been celebrating	the coming and going

of nature's more transient visitors	for years.

They are full of questions	about what will happen next…

As she knows their journey will not be long, she encourages them to harmonize

with her in a symphony of floral music.

The sky is filled with young blooming voices which dance forever in the wind.

Sangita Kalarickal Krivosik
Minnesota
Hour 2

In Frost's Footsteps On A Snowy Evening

the bald eagle that rides the wind,
the rabbit that rushes to hide,
the fox that scurries through,
and the tremolo of the hermit thrush.

Whose woods these are I think I know.

is it the song of my heart,
or the low anguish in my mind?
is it the mere transference
of a gloomy solstice?

The darkest evening of the year.

on simple walks I maneuver,
in wild fancies and fantasies galore.
among bare oaks and maples
and leafless strings of virginia vines.

Of easy wind and downy flake.

I would lie on the pristine snow
no step to mark my reverie,
with long dreams to cherish,
tranquil moments entice.

But I have promises to keep

The highly recognizable lines in italics are from Robert Frost's, 'Stopping By Woods on a Snowy Evening.'

Katrina Moinet
Llanfairpwllgwyngyll, Wales
Hour 7

Solstice

an imperceptible hum of the earth
awakening elsewhere wakes me

pale and milky; night slides the sheen
of a notion past my dimmed eyeline—

I prowl the hedgerows wet with wicker dew
till my narrow pathway beckons to a clearing

and a baritone murmur stays my steps
Derwyddon standing tall and robed in

the mystery of five thousand years
dappled dawn breathes Alban Hefin—

featherlight cloudbursts scatter morning rays
on gathered upturned gazes as we welcome

the new sun

Francis Muzofa
Zimbabwe and Namibia
Hour 3

Epiphany

my walk into the forest
revealed to me harmony in nature
i didn't know that the songs birds sing
are properly choreographed
in unison with the trees

the birds do the vocals
while trees take to the dance floor
the wind is the choirmaster
some trees do percussion
shrubs do the catering
they serve wild berries
on the house

from the blooming flowers
fragrance is awash
it keeps the entire forest fresh and inviting
busy bees make honey
honey for dessert
effortlessly they cross pollinate
nature's processes are properly measured and precisely executed

a rocking rock, was inviting
i took a seat
while enjoying natural air-conditioning
under a big shady tree
i was marvelling at nature and its serenity
until i was forced to take to my heels
        a big green Mamba fell next to me

i didn't regret the forest

        the harmony
        the hospitality
        the tranquility
        the beauty

        ooh! nature you are so wise

nurture us
we have a lot to learn
you have a lot to teach

       please! teach us.

Dan Tighe
Sand Point, Michigan
Hour 9

Elrod Opines

Elrod, the newt, and I talk bluntly,
through the aquarium glass,
about life and living.

He has ideas about food, and I mine, about
what it is like to live in water 24/7.

He loves hamburger, raw. I comment,
"Yuk to that."

I feel the swish of water over my skin, I tell him, as I stroke hard, right/left,
in an aquarium, me-sized, the Australian crawl, I tell him,
but I like to get out, too. Mostly out.

He dives hard, tail-driven,
settles buoyantly upright on the bottom.
He tells me he knows nothing of geography.

"Look," he says, "food, fresh water, companionship,
and of course,
good conversation," he says, "that's all I need."

I think about this, and wonder if he is right,
in a narrowly global sense.

Dave Spinelli
Leadville, Colorado
Hour 6

A deer crossed the road
Antlers covered in velvet
Wiffle ball delayed

Gopalakrishnan Prakash
Hyderabad, India
Hour 12

Captain's Log (A sonnet)

Leafing through the pages of the Captain's log;
of meandering voyages through sea and sand
looking for glimmering light through dense fog
in the dusk's fading hours, relaxing inland.

Assessing the gains and losses of time
skirmishes won and tough battles lost
realizing in the end that life was a mime
straggling at last through the winning post.

Agonies endless have been many a score.
Countless times have I shed bushels of tears,
ecstasies have been not less but more
while haunted by numerous endless fears.

Yet, happily do I set down this song
counting seconds ticking till the final GONG!

Elijah Kinboade
Nigeria
Hour 5

SEEK NO GLORY

Seek no glory when you live,
for you will surely find it when you leave.
Trouble yourself not for fame,
after your departure everyone will know your name.

Speak less of yourself to your fellow men,
when you are gone your loss will be known among women.
Death is a town crier,
raising his voice higher.
Seek not to be recognized by others,
you will surely be known when you obey death's order.

Oliver McKeithan
Milan, Pennsylvania
Hour 7

The Lone Beachcomber

evening sunset, all are gone, I am alone
I enjoy this loneliness
tonight, the sand is mine.

Lexanne Leonard
Centennial, Colorado
Hour 6

My Letter To You

You are a graffitied wall
wondrous, history-laden
marks and words
colors and shapes

All you

Allow more layers
never fear
even if you forget
all that slumbers underneath

The sum will be there
tendering depth, wisdom
protecting the raw

Oh, wondrous graffitied you
ugly and beautiful

Be you

Jill Egland
Bakersfield, California
Hour 3

Technicolor Hills

Technicolor hills
burst into flamingo pink flames and
pierce a cerulean sky
bloodless and leathery
like my arms reaching up
from this 1950s nightmare of hues

finding you cool and updated
in 70s avocado and mauve.
"Toned down," you tell me. But
I see the flicker of something more.
Something incendiary

sleeping in you till one day
the alarm will clatter and
you'll turn your morning the color of
finches; your sky—
jet blue and joyous.

Rebecca Resinski
Conway, Arkansas
Hour 9

fragment from melancholy 9

professing

                                        our

                                                                    perfect

                            entangle

                    m

                              e

                                    n

                              t

*an erasure of a passage from Robert Burton's Anatomy of Melancholy

Tonet Rosales
Philippines

Hour 1

You Will Always Be

I will always
remember you
as a warm summer day

Suffused with
laughter and
bathed in sunshine

You will always be
that way
to me

Even if the
rains come
and the storms
wreak havoc

Janice Mendonca
Melbourne, Australia
Hour 22

Strength and tenderness

Don't let the world convince you that you are weak.
Your tenderness is strength and courage.
Your beauty shines through your soul.
In a world that is constantly defining every little thing
may your tenderness be recognised
as inspiring and joyous
as bold and bright
as raw and pure
as gentle and brave.
May your tenderness keep your heart—

warm and human.

Harvey Schwartz
Bellingham, Washington
Hour 8

Who I Am

I wander through life, a tourist
in my search for sincere, a purist.

Sometimes events are happenstance.
There are times I want to dance
but mostly it's a game of chance.

Be kind to strangers I try to be
knowing it comes back to me.

Keep track of news to some extent
but too much of it can cause torment.

I springboard from securest as
I wander through life, a tourist.

Be kind to strangers I try to be.
Don't come off like a bourgeoisie.
Look in their eyes, not absentee.

And in the end what seals the deal is
show the world my best cartwheel!

Sarah Dittmore
Carnelian Bay, California
Hour 12

Summer Nights Taste Better With You

The juice of a ripe plum rolls down my chin
while the citrus scent of geraniums perfumes the air

Our laughter like fireworks; we paint the sky gold
as the fading fingers of the sun tangle our hair

A choir of crickets underscore stories
shared over peach pie and wine

We welcome the moon as she inches skyward
and do not mourn the loss of sunshine

For we wrap ourselves in blankets
and memories and know that here we are free

To open our hearts, share our scars,
and be all we've ever dreamed we could be.

Pea Flower Tomioka
Singer Island, Florida
Hour 5

Cascade, a tanka

Counting breaths like waves
Crashing lips over my dunes
A fluttered memory,
Full moons like our hips breaking
seaside to our ecstasy.

Shannon Van
Atlanta, Georgia
Hour 11

the spun arms of trees

the spun arms of trees
remind me of yours.

the out-branching of stems
remind me of your hands.

the wind wheezing through the leaves
remind me of your chuckles.

how you heave so brightly,
how the edges of each of your breaths squeak,
how wordy those quick sighs are,
your chest rising and falling in a rhythm.

I hear love escape from the bounds of your lungs,
and the world now has a joy I hope to live in forever.

Caitlin Thomson
Toronto, Ontario
Hour 6

Wedding Planning

We walked through Staples, my hand in yours,
and you said *I want a whole life like this.*

The floor sticky below both of us, I asked,
A whole life in Staples?

Surrounding us were towers of boxed
printer paper, one row over there

were office chairs on shelves, forever
out of reach. An employee walked by

gaze focused on the distant exit.
A life running errands with you,

you said. At the time I dismissed it,
walked fast into the pen aisle

but years later when a friend told me about their
girlfriend drama I said *I'm sorry,*

your relationship would not pass
the Staples test, and I meant

that everyone should be with someone they are
happy doing mundane things with,

no concert trips, or ax-throwing
lessons required.

For over a year we didn't shop with one another

at all, and when we finally stepped

back into a store together, masked,
I understood what you'd said over

a decade ago, differently. It was a
privilege I had undervalued before.

Nishant Jain
Cupertino, California
Hour 7

Together

For that moment,
the entire world disappeared.
It was just her and me,
together in a field.

Alone,
but not lonely.
Silent,
but not silenced.

Every glance was a conversation.
A memory.
A story.
A lifetime.

And it was in what was not said,
that everything was.

Nadiyah Suleiman
Denver, Colorado
Hour 8

Blueberries

Ripe blueberries bounce into my hand
Drops of juice spill over, dripping
Into my mouth, open and gasping
My appetite never quite satisfied
Your touch so gentle and yet prying
Searching for more than I have
More than I am willing to give
But I love blueberries, especially
When they come from you

Daryl Curnow
Auckland, New Zealand
Hour 18

Joy: Then vs Now

It's hard to describe
my feeling of joy
and the randomness of it.
It was a normal day
school holidays were in full swing
then something took over my body
it's often puzzling.
I had always been quite uptight
always wanting to know what was to come
but at this moment
I was in complete bliss.
I climbed the fence
needed to get to the stables
where I'd often talk to the horses
as if they needed a friend.
As my feet hit the ground
I felt a sense of calm and joy
there was no rush, no plans,
just happy to be around.
It's a feeling I have never forgotten
a young boy with the world in front of him.

Twenty-two years on,
the setting has changed
but I have constant joy
it's not a fleeting moment
it's permanent.
No fences needed to be jumped
no horses needed to be spoken to.
Just a girl
and her touch.

Marion Lougheed
Leipzig, Germany
Hour 11

Four on the Floor

We lay, four kids in a square,
one head on each belly,
circuit closed.

"Ha!" you said, and my head bobbed.
"Ha!" I said, and so on round the square.
And round again until our four
heads bobbed and bopped, each
belly breath a pump of air,
a mini-trampoline transmitting
signals to the next link in the chain.

After fifteen or twenty seconds,
message received.
Tidy transmissions
devolved into a bouncing, bopping
concatenation,
cascading vocalizations:
hilarity ensued.

Anne Paterson
Calgary, Alberta
Hour 5

knitting circle

ten am sharp, a knock at the door—twittering voices on the pavement outside.
a turn of the lock, a chain removed—the squeak of the old oak door,
old Bessie was first across the threshold—her ample body filling the space.
Madge, Molly, and Mary, poured in behind her—satchels bursting with needles and wool.
only five today—the others away—Karen, Kathy, Kendra, Kitty absent till Sunday.
hardback chairs with torn leather seats sat upon the rug covered in sunflowers and daisies.
well-padded bottoms settled in place—wine glasses held for fillin',
cheese plate passed from hand to hand—an array of cheddar, mozza, and brie,
whistles wet and bellies sated, the women set to work—instructions tacked to the wall by a nail,
needles ready, wool at their feet—they began.
knit one ladies, purl two and switch, knit two, purl two—next row.
the knitting circle had begun.

Karen Call
Aurora, Colorado
Hour 4

Stairsteps

Their father, James, watched.
They came out of the shack that stood at the dip of the draw
standing, solemn, in a line beside him.
Albert first, though he grumbled about going to school at 15,
then Benjamin, named for his uncle who'd died in the war,
and Caroline, who had green eyes that strangers noticed,
Dancing Deborah as she liked to be called, followed,
then Edward, for James's pa who'd died at the bottom of the mine,
and Frank, who liked to play dress up and hid an old baby doll.
Their mother, Susan, came out last and stood at the end of the line.
She held squirming Georgia in one arm and put
the other hand on the swell of her belly.
The postmistress took their picture. She would
hang it on the wall in the store
and the family would get a copy for Christmas.

Muhammed Ebrahim Suleman
Johannesburg, South Africa
Hour 8

A MOTHER'S LOVE

A mother's love is
something you should
never forget.

A tear rolling down her
cheek, is something that
you should never let

happen— the first person she worries
about is you.

She's someone that you can
count on, even on the days
that you're feeling blue.

She remembers you first in
all of her prayers

and smiles, even through all
of her broken layers.

She gives you her all and
expects nothing in return.

When you are out and about,
sometimes a little
remembrance is all she
yearns.

A mother's love, so pure

and in my opinion, it's the
best cure.

Sheila Sondik
Bellingham, Washington
Hour 3

40th Birthday Poem

---for my firstborn

Her child-sized cello.
How it vibrated
in her embrace.

Her embrace
now overflowing
with three children.

Evelyn Elaine Smith
Waco, Texas
Hour 3

Contrary Dance

City of stars steps out in a counterpoint dance,
giving the night's mellow tones yet another chance,
doubly debonair, what a pair we will make
again, shining once more with the stars until daybreak.

Contrary moods beset us each blessed night,
going from sprightly to methodical
dirge, then back again—now a melodic song—
a sad tune without words, all so deep and strong.

Contrasting moods move us at a lively pace.
Gone is the workaday routine once embraced.
Don't spare caresses! Fill me with your kisses.
A new day dawns, so we don't want to miss it.

John Dutton
Woodbridge, Virginia
Hour 5

Weekend Getaway

Our picnic blanket nestled under the old Oak tree.
My hardback spread across my chest as I nap.
The smell of sunflowers in the air.
My wife is knitting with her back against the tree.
Plates of cheddar cheese and crackers entice us.
Our wine glasses get frequent use.
We let our thoughts drift off into space.
Tomorrow, back on our feet hitting the pavement
fighting tooth and nail to claw out a living.
My satchel bursting with documents and contracts,
but today we rest under the old Oak tree.

Tanya LaForce West
Muncie, Indiana
Hour 4

this moment

lovely evening is upon me
reds, blues, so many hues
clouds rolling across the sky
like waves of the ocean

enjoying every color and tone
forgetting the world is in chaos
how can I stay in this moment
just freeze it and never leave

but no, the world keeps moving
and I along with it

evening is upon me, lovely
so many hues, reds, and blues
rolling across the clouds
waving to the ocean

Nasiha Sadhik
Pondicherry, Kottakuppam, India
Hour 9

9th Cross

With my friends I ride my bicycle,
A time when we all feel delightful.

My aunty is against us riding to 9th Cross,
And warns us not to take that turn,

But once we have planned to go.
So we can buy the yummy, yummy snacks.

While aunty is searching for us,
There we are enjoy eating.

Worried she will find us soon,
We quickly ride back.

Rushing back to the house,
As we were new to it, we forgot the route.

The landmark is a giant blue gate,
We realize that we're lost somewhere.

As I forced my monocled friend to join us,
We had another task to drop her.

While aunty gets ready to search us.
We return home with a prepared lie —

And always 9th Cross,will stay in our hearts.

Uditi Naagar
Chennai, India
Hour 19

Meet 'Trivandrum' – A City in India

A prompt that couldn't be more timely
as I stay in God's own country
streets lively as can be
oh of course, it's the capital city!

For me though, it's so much more
it's my summer vacation
my only connection to the city;
This is where I grew up.

From finishing my handwriting homework
to researching college's coursework
from enrolling in drawing classes
to enrolling in driving classes,
This is where I grew up.

Every vacation,
the zoo, the beach, the museum
the temples, the malls and family friends
oh, there are lists of places to visit.

Different kinds of trees everywhere
coconut trees, banana trees,
trees that are particularly pretty
and the language, well that's just the best

A city with so much more to it
a city whose language is just as pretty
a city I've lived very little in
yet, one that feels so much more like home.

But as I grew, those around me grew too
as my grandparents turn old
as the walls lose their strength
my family decides it's time to let go of the house.

I must tell you before I depart
that this city with its pretty trees,
the people, their language and their culture,
continue to win the hearts of every single visitor.

Confidence Olika
Lagos, Nigeria
Hour 3

"City of Stars"

The city beams and breathes while others sleep
it lights up on weekends—
the bubble spreads like a wildfire.

Alcohol exhumes wild personalities tucked in all week.
Igbo is shared like Communion bread
bodies seek warmth in others
the city is alive and in a high mood.

Saturdays are for Owambe
there's an aunty in yellow—
her face is beat fifty shades lighter
her Gele stands tall
how else do you know she has arrived—
if her Aso-oke doesn't speak hundreds of thousands of naira—
that jewellery is definitely from Dubai.

She orders for Amala
there must be Ogunfe and big fish
those bottles of minerals and malt will find a home in her bag.

Her daughter's waist sits snatched in a corset
this is the hundredth wedding she is attending as an Asoebi girl
but who is keeping count?

Sundays are holy, Sabbath should be kept
now those wild bodies go back to God
with gloomy faces they sit through sermons—
prepared to tuck the wildness into work pants the next day.

While dawn stretches each morning, the city sits wide awake
the scorching sun rises and sets on the backs of the working class—
they sit packed in buses and cars
some shirts billow on bikes avoiding the traffic jam.

The city plays a game of make or break
every sojourner desires to be another star
some give up this hope early

some do not but—
"Eko oni baje."

The five days of the week drag
patiently, like fanatics, they wait to unleash their beasts
faithful in this religion.

Dominique Russell
Toronto, Ontario
Hour 1

Landlocked

The Mediterranean is gone
from me
and with it, youth,
the unadulterated
pleasures of bodies
mine and strangers,
fingertips
on sandy sweat
the grounding fatigue,
waves struggled with
and through, then
the salt-shedding shower
from which emerged,
ghost and flesh
reunited, a goddess
in a white shirt
and the glances
on the rambla
over tapas and sin
cigarettes lit in code,
smoke signals
before the dancing
—oh the dancing!

I miss it,
the sea, the sea, the sea.

Bonnie Katzive
Boulder, Colorado
Hour 8

Rocky Mountain Reflection

"Over the place where Long's Peak and its slightly less imposing companions stand in lofty isolation and invite the summer tourist to their cool retreats, the waves of an open sea once rolled and its tide ebbed and flowed, unhindered by rock or shoal" (NPS.gov).

Meadows swim: yellow, periwinkle, and green
framing curlicues of snaking streams
washing down from the mineraled mountain.
I touch an icy, bubbling flow and salts eroded from ancient glacial slabs
coat my finger, connecting me to those upswept ocean floors.

The sea is now the sky,
tides of air directing clouds like swells,
reflections wafting through the horseshoe streams
fastening clouds back to earth,
mirrors interrupted rhythmically by waving grasses
until it all feels

like an ancient weaving
like time turned over
like I have always walked here.

Kevin J. O'Conner
Bellingham, Washington
Hour 12

Pulse

Ultimately
it is the center
around which everything revolves

slowing
quickening
sometimes skipping or stuttering

but always relentless—
from start to finish

We may fall out of step
or go astray
but we always come back

Because the drum is everything

Jennifer Faylor
Everett, Washington
Hour 4

Everyday Music

There is music in any moment
if I listen. Notes are written
in invisible ink, spelling out
what even my ancestors knew to be true.

The clock is a metronome for today's melody.
I press the pedal of awareness
to deepen the sound,
tighten the glowing strings that stretch
across my whole being
and the bow of existence
glides over me
echoing a simple symphony
through the caverns of time.

Lost… and Found
(Liberties, Connections, Hope, Time)

"The great art of life is sensation, to feel that we exist, even in pain."

Lord Byron

Nykki Norlander
Morgan, Minnesota
Hour 2

Music

The woods are lovely, dark and deep.
I whisper my secrets to the leaves.
Time is lost and I am found.
I'm not alone among the creatures who sleep,
as I face the demons in my mind.
The wind creates music within the trees.
And we dance together long past evening.

* *'The woods are lovely, dark and deep', Robert Frost*

Darryl Commings
St. Louis, Missouri
Hour 12

I Dissent

"When one group breaks the covenant of truth and assumes an exclusive role in defining the basis of human relationship, that group plants the seed of rebellion."

–James H. Cone. Black Theology and Black Power (1969)

It will never be anything other than

> an uneasy balancing act
> between us

That is the condition and cost

We tell stories of temptation

> it slithers and sheds its skin
> it sounds reasonable to reasonable people

Or, for dramatic effect, we set the desirable thing

> behind a chain link fence
> we poke our fingers between the links

We dream the dreams of petty tyrants

> whose bellies and hearts are never full
> and the soul of this world is never enough

Temptation is real

This world is built on a promise
Not a statue
Our bodies require bonds that are renewed daily

The claim is a simple one...

I am a living being...

> with living beings...

on a living being...

And so are you

To be is to make that claim
To be held to that claim
To be judged by that claim

We live a circular scale

> or maybe a spiral
> to understand this is to understand justice...

Not just a word we say

> but a living template

> > a claim made on each other just because we are alive...

A claim I hope and expect
You will make of me
As I make of you

When you get drunk with power…
I dissent.

Christina Tang-Bernas
Anaheim, California
Hour 10

kind-ness

it is a radical thing
for a human to be kind
we with the genocidal genetics
of the Homo Sapiens who wiped out
the Neanderthals, the Denisovans
the mammoths and giant sloths
a million other species
anything we did not consider
worth our own kind
whose ancestors fought wars
for any kind of difference in the way
we looked or talked or believed
the words: not like us, not our kind
woven through our shared history
for to be kind is to generate empathy
for someone not us
to look at another
who is not myself
and think they deserve to be treated
as I deserve to be treated
to choose to look past differences
accept they are my kind
we are of a kind
there is a kind-ness here between us
and extend a hand forward

Abioye Aisha
Abuja, Nigeria
Hour 2

Listen, It's The Sound of Fury

Call me truth.
For I am the most elusive captive,
a friend of sun.
I dabble in the blood of my enemies
& pacify my skin
with the vanquish of my foes.
You see, I have travelled
through the clouds of hell –
earth's flames have little meaning
to this black vessel.
My head bangs the galaxies
and my feet are on the mountains.
I know too well of the heavens,
even your chi
is my ally.

*Chi – God

Chidozie Chukwubuike
Nigeria
Hour 5

In the World of the Wealthy

In the world of the wealthy pavements are plated in gold. No one intrudes into another's space and there is time to admire sunflowers.

On the flip side of the class divide, garbage heaps adorn the streets.

Everyone bumps into everyone, and fights with stones and nails are a sacred ritual in the struggle to maintain an equilibrium of backwardness.

In that cocoon of affluence where the rich converge to dine, wine glasses are of the most exquisite and tasteful kind.

But the poor are also there, in their arena of poverty, jostling over the leftovers abandoned by the menacing dogs of the wealthy.

In the world of the rich the code is to keep raising the equilibrium point for success.

Hafeezah Yates
Summerville, South Carolina
Hour 5

Guided Path

Along the path to enlightenment,
we encounter life's highs and lows.
Mere survival and determination become a mantra.
Acquiring the physical, emotional, spiritual, and mental strength
to surpass primitive understanding.

Ancestral guides try to periodically download pieces
of a mastered blueprint into our memory.
Thoughts clouded by the 24 hours in a day, we only hear static.
Bound by their songs of redemption,
we tend to rest but not sleep.

Haunted by the chains they wore in bondage.
Through the days, months, and years with limited tears we press forward.
Resurfacing a new breath of light within our disconnected souls.
Embracing the balance of self-mastery
as the fallacies of the world unfold.

Tazeen Fatma
Jodhpur, India
Hour 12

déjà vu
I mind map
reality

Ananya Panwar
Mumbai, India
Hour 12

Gathered for Massacre

The harvest was ripe and gold
What a gathering to behold
The sky was gay, and colors merry
A romantic pink, a scarlet cherry

All gathered to celebrate
Sweat of toil – but fickle fate
Had something else in store
Shrieks of pain, cries of gore

Rain showered them with grain
Bullets fired shooting pain
Groups of innocents huddled in fear
To jump in wells or swallow tears
Children sobbed and clung to breasts
Mother's stricken, men were prest

But Dyer kept on firing
His selfish heart, ne'er tiring
Like a bloodbath it poured
Silence resounding ever more
Rivers of shame, of ghastly pain
Would not claim such unjust gain
Blooming blood of innocents slain
Booming guns – horrific refrain

No matter what time, what the place
This hardened brutal truth I face
'twas nothing but a glaring preface

To a bloody

heartless

massacre

*The reference here is to the Jallianwala Bagh Massacre of 13th of April 1919

Solape Adeyemi
Mowe, Ogun, Nigeria
Hour Unknown

A Folklore: Iginla the Great King

He was fearless and brave
known throughout the seven kingdoms
for his prowess and skill
he was never afraid to fight on the battlefield
to protect the territorial integrity of his kingdom
wise and knowledgeable
he was sought for miles
but, the great Iginla trusted too much and too soon
he trusted his second in command
a man who had proven himself faithful, time and time again
unfortunately,
you cannot tell the mind's construction from the face
for his second in command after a while
began to nurse ambitious ideas of his own
he thought he would not could make a better King
and so, treacherous thoughts flooded his heart and mind
until eventually he made a pact with the enemies of the kingdom
And then,
akin to the fate of the great Julius Caesar
who was slain by Brutus, 'his protégé', and others,
King Iginla was slain
one cold rainy night on his bed.
And his second in command, Ifira, the betrayer, reigned in his stead.

Lavinia Leon
Calgary, Alberta, Canada
Hour 3

MappaMondrian

wouldn't it be at least unsettling
to awaken under a backbending crimson tree
it would wonder who painted you
maybe branch out, reach out to its friends
debate on where you may have come from
put you in a museum of curiosities
curated by emissaries who transited your world
like Mondrian

Gita Bharath
Chennai, India
Hour 22

Bird's Eye-View

How insignificant are these things
depending on wheels,
or on metal wings.
Moving along pre-set ways,
unable to grasp, to understand
the immensity of the sky.
I ride an updraft, glide on high,
spot with my stereoscopic eye
a red car stopped beside the freeway.
Maybe the driver has slowed his pace
to take in the beauty of nature's grace
of the greensward or the trees.
I can move any which way
in the sky, my 3D space,
the sun on my feathers
the wind in my face
and so I pity

....

the earth-bound human race.

Sue Storts
Tulsa, Oklahoma
Hour 1

Shadow of the Tower

Tai chi in Central Park,
shadow of Trump Tower
near Columbus Circle.
Congressional witnesses disclose
White House corruption.
Empty wine bottle on bench
proclaims last night's debauchery,
as rodents found refuge.
Brazen little brown mouse
scampers between our feet
asking for some reciprocity,
some quid pro quo.
"How about I don't crawl up your leg,
you drop me some food."
We play in Central Park,
home to mobster mice,
guarded by monuments to evil men.

Melody Pender
Lagos, Nigeria
Hour 12

I Saw

I saw you last year on the news;
you were the one clothed in blue and gray, you were the one whose smile seemed fake,
you were the one who had a sad eye on a happy face,
you were the one who shed unseen tears,
you were the one who wanted to be free, you were the one who lied and said you're fine.

I saw you last year on the news.

I saw you last month at the show;
you were the one with an aching heart but no one could tell,
when I approached you my name didn't ring a bell,
you were the one inwardly dying and outwardly laughing,
you were the one saying hopeful things to others — things that you really wanted someone to tell you.

I saw you last month at the show.

I saw you last week at the mall;
you were the one with sunken eyes but glaring makeup on,
you were the one carrying so many bags they became burdens,
you were the one looking at the distorted mirror,
you were the one moving with a crowd of fake friends.

I saw you last week at the mall.

I saw you last night;
you were the one crying at 3am,
you were the one that screamed aloud from a nightmare,
you were the one walking down the street in the dead of night... feeling no cold as your heart was all frozen up,
you were the one wishing it was all over, you were the one going through your masks — trying to decide which one to put on the next

    morning.

I saw you last night.

I saw you at the bar six hours ago;
you were the one holding a glass of champagne,
you were the one with bloodshot eyes and a miserable smile,
you were surrounded by cameras,
you were the one not living life, but existing.

I saw you at the bar six hours ago.

I walked by your house just now;
you had a stemmed glass in your hand and an open wine bottle nearby,
you rocked your head to an R&M beat, your eyes were shut but you could see things through your mind's eye — things were falling apart around you but you didn't care,
you just shut your eyes and drowned beneath the waves of the song.

Then you opened your eyes and saw me.

Maritza M. Mejia
Florida
Hour 6

We Are Not Strangers

sometimes we feel we are the only ones,
until we travel and find…
new people and cultures.

sometimes we feel we're trapped inside ourselves
until we realize…
there are other doors to go out.

sometimes we stay in our comfort zones,
until we open our eyes...
to another way of life.

sometimes we think death is the end,
until we learn…
it's the beginning.

sometimes we need to stop and reflect,
until we realize…
we are not strangers

Diana Kristine
Dallas, Texas
Hour 5

The Sunflowers Grow

She waits beneath the old oak
knitting as she floats in a sea of sunflowers.

They were only seeds once,
but the sunflowers grew.

She waits.

A round table just noticeable above the green and yellow has been set beside her,
just the right size for two but too large for only one.
She waits
and the sunflowers grow.

The wheel of once fresh cheese has turned to mold,
and the rich liquid in the wine glass soured long ago.
She waits
and the sunflowers grow.

They are watered by her tears
and undisturbed by her sorrow.

Her face has wrinkled, her eyes have dimmed,
still, she waits
and the sunflowers grow.

She doesn't know
he never received her letter.
She wonders if he forgot her
and he wondered that too.

He will not come, though she won't believe
he never looked for her under the great tree.
Instead, his sorrow consumed him, and he is gone.

Still, she waits
watching the sunflowers grow.

Adam Lipscomb
Austin, Texas
Hour 6

The cicada nymph slowly climbs

along the branch, inch by
laborious inch. It has taken most
of the afternoon, and as the sun
begins to set, it stops.

"Is it resting?" I wonder to myself,
then I see it shiver and crack
and slowly, painfully, it
emerges – wings wet and
furled, shell soft and white.

Ever so slowly, wings unroll
carapace hardens and
becomes glittering green

until, as the stars rise above,
it spreads its wings and flies away.

"Godspeed, little friend," I whisper,
as I finish packing the last box
of my past and prepare to rest.

Tomorrow, I begin a new life
without you in it

Stefanie Hutcheson
Lenoir, North Carolina
Hour 6

Well, hey there, Stefanie! I know we've been out of touch for a while now, but I occasionally see your face pop up when some of our mutual acquaintances have tagged you. When it does, my heart bleeds.

I'm going to be honest here. It's hard, so please forgive me if my words don't come out right. Not to be honest overall, but—to be honest with you. You are the type of person who demands honesty, and, frankly, it scares me. Which is part of why I stopped being in your world. We don't see eye to eye on certain things, and—unfortunately for our once wonderful friendship—those things mean more to me than you did. How's that for honesty?

I'm not trying to be mean here. You deserve an explanation for why I bolted. You were a true friend to me, and I still think of those car rides to Charlotte when we bared our souls to each other. When I see Tom's Barbecue Chips, I remember how you bought me a bag and opened it from the bottom, telling me the best chips were always found there. You knew I had OCD and that this drove me crazy, but you risked it because you are such a funny girl.

I miss you. I see you on Facebook; see your books around the local bookstores. I look for posts from the writing group and upcoming events you all might be sponsoring or participating in. Those were some great times and I miss being a part of them. Sometimes I think about coming back…

…but how would you react? I mean, I made you a promise—a pinky promise—and I failed to keep it. Would you give me a second chance? Would you allow me the opportunity—the privilege—of loving you once more? Or would our conflicts separate us again?

Dare I find out? You really are a lovely person, Stef. Can I let go of my pride and love the whole of you without always liking those parts that made me leave to begin with? Are we worth another chance, as Barry Manilow sings that song right now about being ready? Am I ready to take a chance again? What have I to lose? What have I to gain?

Silly me. Of course you would welcome me back. Probably you'd say something cute, like, "Hey, Love! Turn around a moment." Puzzled, I would acquiesce, and then you'd say, "It's so good to see you're back."

(You do love those double-entendres, don't you, Stef?). Then you'd laugh, I'd laugh, and the air would be clear, just like that.

The chances are good that we wouldn't even speak of this prolonged break because I know you, Stefanie. I know you. I know you still love me, that you didn't stop, and that you've been hoping for this—even though I didn't return your calls or respond to your messages. I know you, Stefanie. I know your hopeful heart is waiting for one move, one gesture from me. What I don't know is if I can make it.

Oh, heart! I want to! I miss you so much! And the stories we have to tell one another are enough to involve many more trips to Charlotte, the waterfall you once took me to, or any of the places we explored on our twenty or more dates.

In closing, don't give up on me. I don't think I am ready just yet, but…I implore you: don't write me off just yet. What? You haven't? I assumed as much.

Thank you, Stefanie.

Soon…

Denise Hill
Bay City, Michigan
Hour 4

what we wrought

2122
it's quiet again
the machines quelled
as night falls
we each sit
in silent solitude
looking out over
barren terrain
hopeful
tomorrow may rain
regenerate something
anything
but the forecast
likely disagrees
decades gone by
at least it hasn't ended
not entirely
not yet

Anna Cavouras
Toronto, Canada
Hour 11

Dragon Breath

The Vancouver sky turned red the summer of two thousand and fifteen.
I held my newborn and gulped precious water
trying to clear the ash from my tongue.

The toddler in my house tested my patience.
Over and over with this and with that
as we stayed inside day after day.

Temperatures high, tempers short.
Heat inside and out, the ferocity
of a dragon building inside of me.

The collective inhale and exhale like a dragon full of fire.
Heat on everyone's breath, air burning, ash raining,
water elusive.

This is all summers now.

Fire season is a new season, slipped into the calendar.
Every year longer and hotter than the last.

Is there a temperature at which it will stop?

Water evaporates long before it reaches the flame.
Parched ground. Tinder-dry grass. Everything is thirsty.
Climate destruction unchecked.

Inhale.

Exhale.

Gasp.

Ana Marie Dollano
NCR, Philippines
Hour 15

Empty Leaves

empty leaves
adrift—
a certain sadness

Valarie Kirkwood
Topeka, Kansas
Hour 7

Invasion of the Lilies

Five years ago frustrated and longing for beauty, I dug beneath the rocks to bury bulbs for Lilies into the fertile ground.
The rocks I had placed with a flustered pace but soon they commenced to fade.
Fragrant heads of blossoms I envisioned looming to conceal the faded pebbles at their feet.
This year Stargazer, Oriental Lilies sprang up as if overnight.
Trumpet lilies stood lanky above them in colors sublime and bright.
Golden in hue they were, pink with variegated trumpets.
Hot pink and fuchsia star shaped blooms.
They lined the front of the house like Disney Princesses on parade.
But summer is here and as it marches towards fall, their laces and sashes all
droop and fade.

Wendie Donabie
Bracebridge, Ontario (Muskoka Region)
Hour 5

HOPE

In the space,
between the pavement
and the bomb-levelled home,
the oak tree clung to life,
its limbs splintered
by shrapnel.

Beside it a solitary sunflower,
its face bent in sorrow,
looked down at a wine glass -
shattered.

Nature grieves for us,
yet hopes
for an end to war.

Diane Carmony
La Quinta, California
Hour 4

Playing piano for the last time (Ukraine)

Amid the chaos and cruelty of war,
amid the bombings, the fires,
amid the desperate attempts to flee,
amid the broken glass, smashed pots,
abandoned belongings,
the woman uncovers her beloved piano,
wipes the dark dust from the keys,
and then,
for the last time,
the very last time,
she sits down in her coat and hat and
she plays,
her hands floating across the keys,
creating notes of hope and peace
to fill the shattered home that
she now must leave behind.

Nancy Canyon
Bellingham, Washington
Hour 7

CROWNED ROCKET BIRD

flies for three days above the speckled salvia,
a field of red, the queen returns home.

she is fast, thus her name Rocket Bird
and colorful with orange wings and yellowgreen
body. she flies on, unrelenting in her journey.

you come every day to watch for her, like the flicker
you know her call, *chena chena peep*, soaring over the fields,
up the silent valley, winging toward twilight.

as though she shows you the way.
as though you seek the vanishing point as well.

Amy Joy Bostelman
Leander, Texas
Hour 5

A Question Without an Answer

A question without an answer—
Ivory towers

a space full of hardbacks
fills the brim of satchels struggling
to stay stitched together

Attempts at knitting theories
the promise of "the Answer",

enticing academics towards the
trap with cheddar cheese

A thirst that won't be quenched

no matter how much fills
the wineglass

How can it be explained
that Miracles still exist?

Like the sunflower growing through a crack in pavement
and the resilience of the oak seedling striving for growth where
it shouldn't be.

Shrehya Taneja
Delhi, India
Hour 11

surviving

the twisted tree is hit by the storm
grandma forgets me
but remembers the young sapling
right outside her home
she checks on it hourly
but walks carelessly to her bed
getting scrapes
she asks me questions
gives me names that she likes

the twisted tree survives the storm
she lavishes love and affection on the survivor

my grandma still does not remember me

the storm in our house rages on

Sandy Lender
Central Florida
Hour 3

Lapwings on the Moors

the clouds settled early
over the moors today
reminding me
of the frosts
coating the late lapwing eggs
nestled in the nest

thus I ran
I ran to gather them
to protect them
to save them
to give them
a warm place they might shelter
during a cold night

only to find you'd tortured them
with your trap

a trap I now see
your bars revealed to me
I long to escape your hold
thus I run
lest I die nestled in the nest

Rhea Kumar
Cupertino, California
Hour 1

Underwater Grounding

As I go through each day these days, I am greeted by
a flurry of emails, To-Do lists, errands.
I try to tackle each task but then
I pause.

I imagine the water, all around me, clear and blue,

weighing me down by its heaviness.
Slowly, it blocks out the outside world
till it's just me and the blue and the water
and silence.

As I sit, trying my hardest to breathe,

I begin to notice:
The blue in the water, and how it changes to light.

Its coolness enveloping my arms and face, the freshness soothing my tongue.
The silent whooshing sounds of the waves above.

Bubbles leaving my nose as

I breathe.

The water feels heavy no more.
I take a deep breath in; my legs move on will.

And to the surface
I rise.

Joy M. Winstead
Mogadore, Ohio
Hour 4

Time is Forever

Old man waiting
for inspiration to strike
the keys,
like lightning.

BOOM!

The piano turns to dust; the man to ash.
Time is heartless, unforgiving

The spirit of man and piano,
will forever be in the forest primeval,
haunting those not yet born.

Allison Douglas-Tourner
Victoria, British Columbia, Canada
Hour 8

Calling

The waves are full of blue sky and cedar –
the tide halfway out – the stones slippery
with kelp and fat fingered bladderwrack
I pick my way into the cold water
The gravel basin of the bay is half full –
my swimming pool smaller and closer today
To the right a low granite cliff stands between
sun and sea – darkening the water
Its stoic influence wraps around my body
sedate, mysterious – and
I am drawn into stillness
as if by some internal tide –
of loneliness that is not at all sad

Teresa Locascio
Santa Cruz, California
Hour 6

Love Always, Your Freshman Year Biology Teacher

To the most disruptive girl in class
the one who had to be separated
from her friends to pay attention
and then became sad and shut down

rather than bright and engaged
I see you finally fulfilling that potential
we spoke about so many times
I know I was never your favorite
and I appreciated the letter you wrote me
long after you'd graduated and gone and
just know that
although I'm not sure what it would mean to you,
you've
made
me
proud.

Halle Hund
Eden Prairie, Minnesota
Hour 11

Meliae

Drops of iron soak into the earth,
giving you your first breath.
Roots anchor you to your mother,
knotted wood encases your spirit.
From your limbs, flowers bloom,
bringing with them companions of bees and birds.

You will never know your father,
but one day you will learn how he died at his son's hands.

Maxine Wise
Ottawa, Canada
Hour 8

Skin Deep

I've grown numb to beauty
preaching its worth from the shallows.

Making a neat fist I shatter
my vanity mirror, watching
the shards fall into non-existence.

Perhaps I'll start a revolt against
all the mirrors so eager

to define our worth from
one careless reflection given.

Society's afraid of me telling girls that
I've grown numb to beauty.

Perhaps I'll start a revolt against
my alter ego. Will happily lock
the box myself as I

rise to the sun where I belong,
beautiful in my imperfect skin.

Aisha Nazir
Denver, Colorado
Hour 8

Home

This is a little bit of a story, a little bit of a poem
a little bit of my mom's chai that I can never get right,
a little bit of my dad's books; those I always got right,
but sometimes they would have rippled pages,
because my mom threw them in the water once when he came home late—
Just a bucket of water, that ate
all the words
she never said anything to us, her children,
though I think she suspected he loved his books more?
Someone must love us more
except, love is tricky, and muddy,
and dusty, and I'm allergic
to dust.

So loving me was never easy
and hiding that was difficult, I suspect
and if nothing else was hidden, I hid
under books and music, and broken container lids
that were always too familiar but never enough.
Like pain is when you grow old with it.
I could never sit,
And so I sailed myself away, as one does.

Trust
the process – as is in baking and cooking, and sewing, and sweeping.
None of which I ever learnt;
I guess then my fingers were almost always burnt.
And no other chai tasted like home,
except 'home to me is wherever you are,'
so home should be, where I am?
But I remembered too late that I never liked chai
until I left.

Rashmi S Kurup
Kerala, India
Hour 15

What If?

She said, "Hold your tongue!
Only speak when you are spoken to."
What if I have my opinion?
She said, "You have to be flexible. That
which doesn't bend is broken." What if I
refuse to break?
She said, "Be his shadow;
never step ahead of him."
What if I want to have my own existence?
She said, "Forget your past;
start anew with no luggage from the past."
What if I want to cling on to my childhood?
What if I want to break this chain?
What if I don't carry it generation after generation?
I want my girls to be free.
Never change for anyone.
Find someone who accepts them as they are.

Zainab Suleiman
Denver, Colorado
Hour 2

Marshmallows

Crackling of wood
The embers flying
Five sticks
Five marshmallows
Burning, melting
Falling into the flames
Unattended

Janelle Hershberger
Stow, Ohio
Hour 1

Lake

Intense, piercing sun rays
scorch the thick air;
boiling through this sultry summer day.
Sunbeams violently grab the water
shooting back into the rich sapphire sky,
like brilliant fireworks.
Glassy waves wash up;
leaving remnants of memories…
The lake will always be his favorite.

Gena Williams
Lenoir, North Carolina
Hour 5

Memory

She looked up from her knitting
at her daughter sprawled on the carpet
reading a hardback copy
of "Nail in the Oak Tree."

Taking a sip from her wine glass,
she popped a cracker
and a cube of extra-sharp cheddar cheese
into her mouth.

At the window, the twilight beckoned her.
"I'm going out to water the sunflowers.
Wanna come? It's pretty out."

"Sure." The girl marked her page
and slid the book into her satchel.

Outside, they stood on the driveway pavement
discussing whether there was space
in this flower bed for the zinnias they had bought,
or would they be happier somewhere else?

Arms around each other,
they spent several amiable minutes
admiring the garden, the fireflies,
and the moon-filled night.

Their last evening together.

Britton Gildersleeve
Blacksburg, Virginia
Hour 8

Neo-gigan for a Roc

They might have been eggs   pebbles of sodalite or chalcedony
nestled within wooden cups   three and four to a family

It's what they looked like: eggs lain by some prehistoric bird
bright of wing and long of beak, legs drawn up like cranes might
soaring over unmapped lands long since lost to me

While the fierce mother of these unhatched rocs (mythic, stifled)
waits somewhere in another era, a timeline far removed from now.

She broods, a harpy eagle of sorts, her face not quite human
not quite avian. She is other, mother of rocks that once were eggs

now metamorphosed into stone, pebbles that should have been eggs
unresponsive to a soft whirring of wings.

In this fierce mother's world, there is no mythic partner to mourn with her
only the cacophony of a forest I will never know, although her solitary
state is familiar. I too await misfortune on my own, now.

And the small bluegreen stones that once held the possibility of light
nestle still in wooden hollows that are all they will remember of a home.

Angela Theresa Egic
Astoria, New York
Hour 1

Watery Dream

I dreamt of her again
I dreamt of water again
It was flowing over my feet.

Mom, come save me!
Before it rises above my head.

It never did.

It only rose knee high.
It was smooth . . .
gentle . . .
warm . . .
. . . it was her.

I could still walk through the watery waves.
But where would I go?

I'd rather drown in her warmth.

Be enveloped in it.
Float on it . . .
Be in it . . .
Then to be without it.

Mom, come back, please.

Rumbi Chen
Australia
Hour 6

The One I Was

I want to dance to this song
with the one who wooed my heart
who knows,
perhaps, but my mind was blinded by folly
reason not fully comprehending
the illusion it could be
dilution of the senses
decision of one's worth
my worth
a battle of three worlds – of three words
I miss you

Farzana Suleman
Johannesburg, South Africa
Hour 2

TO THE BOY

There is a boy I had once known.
Who was always quiet and always alone.
He never had friends and never would talk.
He always kept his head down when he would walk.

I never spoke to him or tried to be his friend.
But I somehow knew he had scars to mend.
So maybe "known" is not the word that should be used
because "knowing" and "know of" must not be confused.

Sometimes I wonder about him even though it's been years.
What was the reason behind his unshed tears?
Why was it that he always seemed down?
What was the cause of his constant frown?

Years later I wish I had at least flashed him a smile
or even offered him a simple "hello" once in a while.
Too dumb and stupid I was back then;
the naivety that comes from being in grade ten.

So to the boy who always covered his face
know that I wish I had given you just one embrace.
You are still thought about to this day
and wherever you are, I hope you are okay.

Renae Ogle
Phoenix, Arizona
Hour 6

Triad Letter: The Family

My darling daughter,

When I left the house that New Year's Day,
I ended up dying.
Thought I was indestructible,
but the highway got me in the end.

We never said goodbye.
I can only imagine how a loss
so abrupt made its home
inside your developing psyche.

Your mom must have been in shock,
then she had to give birth.

Must have been awful.
I'm so very sorry.

Love Dad

Daughter,

He left me too, you know.
that New Year's Day…
alone with two children and
a half-finished house.
I was blinded by rage, so I nurtured
you and took it out on your
brother while you watched
helpless, powerless.

Then later, I denied all.
Years go by and I've grown
very old.

You take me in and
never outwardly

blame me —after
all your brother came out

broken; I couldn't handle him.
What was I supposed to do?

But…I had a peaceful
end.

I'm sort of sorry.

Mom

Renae,

When I died, I was angry.
I blamed you—you left and
never looked back.
They put me in the state hospital;
made me a zombie.

You tried to visit I know but
She controlled that too.

I'm with them now and I
have peace—
you should too.

There was nothing you could have done.

She was not self-aware,
She couldn't love me.

You did. I know that now.
And…You took away gifts from

this and now use them to help

others - keep doing that

And be at peace sister.

Love Paul

Junior Knight
Coos Bay, Oregon
Hour 15

"The Lights Are On, Despite The dark"

It is the dead of night,

i sit in awe of the noises
still being made.
No filters on the reverberations.
Exhaust echoing off the now cool black top.

Tires spinning too fast as brakes pump.

The chirp of nightingales
playing holler back.
Even the dew seems to whistle
as it drips from top to bottom leaf.

The spark of my lighter
triggers tracer memories
bonfire dances, in the moonlit dark.

Before i let myself question
the bickering laughter of siblings
awake long after the sun has left,
i remind myself the neighbor is terminal.
While i am busying myself, trying to hush my memories
and drift to sleep...
they are trying to squeeze as many memories as will fit within a second.

i whisper prayers from the shadows of my porch...

"If it be to your purpose Lord,
might you grant the unspoken wishes
hidden in the laughter coming from these wounded hearts."

KV Adams
Melbourne, Victoria, Australia
Hour 13

THE GIFT

The winter sun warms my lap as it inches slowly upwards to embrace me.
The dew whimpers goodbye as it dries on faux grass, and the border plants wave
in the breeze at the waning crescent moon, who in her desire for more time
with her distant lover the sun, lingers to look longingly at him in the clear blue sky.

As I sit on the porch drinking chai, watching my suburban street come alive
I realise I've finally arrived at a time and space I never thought would eventuate;
a time where you're just a memory and the heartbreak of unrequited love
is treasured for the profound gift it was.

Brian Hasson
Derry City, Northern Ireland
Hour 2

Choices

Between the woods and frozen lake
neither path I wish to take
For survival I must choose one
I'll wait for the arrival of the sun.

The sun rises, my path still not clear
no steps taken; I'm trembling with fear
The lake's surface covered with Ice and Snow
however, the strength of it I do not know.

The trees in the woods whisper, "Come, this way."
Beautiful in appearance, can I trust what I hear them say?
I'll close my eyes; slowly breathe in
how did I get here, how did it begin?

Between the woods and frozen lake
which path should I take?
Should I open my eyes and let out a scream?
Maybe I'll awaken, hoping it was a dream

Opening line is from 'Stopping by woods on a Snowy Evening', by Robert Frost

Tessa Mountain
Ambler, Pennsylvania
Hour 3

Sanctuary

sunlight sparkles in dust motes
sent swirling by a stray wingflap
ancient stone floors tap-tap-tap
mutedly under layers of moss and leaf

the wooden pews have rotted soft
chipmunks and robins their only visitors
light enough to rest on the weakened benches
and comprehend nothing of religion

ivies and wildflowers peek around walls
cautiously sneaking over the floor
exploring their discovered ruins
with all the time in the world

a pulpit and altar stand still
keeping stewarding watch
over the greening sanctuary
and the mice that nest there

all this splayed beneath a bright rainbow glow
casting golden amber, ruby, sapphire, emerald
between the shadows of swaying branches
from the crumbling stained-glass window

Paul Sarvasy
Bellingham, Washington
Hour 6

A Question

a golden shovel after Cecilia Meireles

How do we weigh the sounds between I
and thou that enable us to hear
all of the vowels and consonants the
voices vying for our attention in this world
are trying to keep us from sobbing
in despair so we can ground ourselves like
an ancient bristlecone pine rooted in a
hostile environment that seems foreign
and yet is embedded in our own language

Julianne Abend
Hewlett, New York
Hour 6

(Hashtag)#AnotherMomentInLife

Hashtag – I'm awesome!
Hashtag – It's my birthday month!
Hashtag - Photo creds of selfies: by me
wait for it...
Hashtag - Guess what I just read on Reddit? A story about me! P.S. I may have written and posted that story, just now.
Hashtag, Hashtag, h-a-s-h-t-a-g – I'm bored…
or maybe come up for air, for giving a smile, for human kind, to care, to love, to be more than a photo, blog, blurb, bout of selfness that only feeds it's id...
"What ID? My passport photo is soooo bad. The lightening was off." filters everywhere –
Hashtags end words now?
Juxtapose the id hashtag and the supercool - I mean - superego h-a-s-h-t-a-g.
It's reality, my friends –
another moment in life.

Tiffany V. Thomas
Cornelius, North Carolina
Hour 1

Carbon

Shimmering, steely, slick
Rain cuts the air
In heavy sheets

Heavens determined
To wash away the carbon pieces
Turned terribly wrong

The element has evolved
Into a most awful version
Of itself

Electrons outnumbering protons
The six and six and six
Has become unstable

The storm will persist
Until each particle finds its charge
Until the carbon stabilizes

Until it learns to love again

Katelyn Dunne
Chicago, Illinois
Hour 1

After all

    this

    time

      and   are

                                                      stars   any

all   only   more

  these   my

             where

turns   know

       don't

  I

*This poem is in the shape of the Pisces Constellation

Bella Ogwuche
Abuja, Nigeria
Hour 12

Haunted

The wind tonight carries heavy waves   and I wonder

if in any way I can withstand them.   The water also

carries a familiar face

maybe not so familiar.

This night we sit side by side   burn our incense

throw it to God   hope they don't return the same way.

Maria Riofrio
New York City, New York
Hour 9

Identity

I am a mathematician
my world is made up of equations
of how to navigate people
not toward, but around,
accelerating the calculus
of a life divisible by one.

I am a survivalist
relying on the fundamentals
to keep me whole
but they lack
the additions and subtractions
of a fulfilled existence.

I am an actor
but not a very good one apparently
because you, dear friend,
who bears the weight of my well-rehearsed deception
sees through the performance
and I am scared to death
that you'll walk out of the theater
and leave me alone
with my monologue.

I stand still
and let the planet revolve around me
making no attempt
to plunge into its chaotic orbit.

If I could, like a baby,
take that first step
flying forward
the pure strive, the reach
on instinct alone
from a primal desire
to simply be in the world,
would you stay and watch me soar?

Poetics
(Poets, And the Art of Poetry)

"Poets are the hierophants of an unapprehended inspiration; the mirrors of the gigantic shadows which futurity casts upon the present; the words which express what they understand not; the trumpets which sing to battle, and feel not what they inspire; the influence, which is moved not, but moves. Poets are the unacknowledged legislators of the world."

Percy Bysshe Shelley, A Defence of Poetry

Linda Hallstrom
Sioux Falls, South Dakota
Hour 12

The Gathering

We gather at our regular table
in a used bookstore.

What a fine idea that they sell wine
along with books
and schedule poetry readings
and trivia nights.

What a blessing
that I know women
who love wine and books and trivia.

Women who drive downtown
once a week to find parking
and drink wine
and inhale the scent of books.

How lucky to know women
who prefer cozy places
away from the 'in crowd.'

Women who value conversation
and laughter
and friendship.

Women without an agenda
or pretense—

The women who gather
at our regular table
in a used bookstore.

Melissa McCarter
Yonkers, New York
Hour 2

Moonflower

I bury grief in my bones and walk
so someday you will have a poem
about a flower that opens
its face at dusk—no one passes by
to smell the heavy sweetness linger.
Under the moon, flowers pure
and white climb the fence
to what shines above.
I think they too want to hold
the hand of God before closing.
Only you see it now
through me. Others lose faith
in the flower, the moon,
in God.

Mildred Achoch
Nairobi, Kenya
Hour 20

ECHO HUSBAND

Come here, Poem.
Lie with me.
Lie to me.
Lie in me.
Lie that my echo husband is real.
Lie that every lie I feel
is water under a rickety bridge.
Lie that ones and zeroes
can turn an online ogre into a home-bound hero.
Lie that this dark, dank cave
is a palmy, balmy tropical island,
full of flowers and flirting
with wedding waves.
Lie with me on this bed of roses.
No, leave my rose-coloured glasses
and top hat
on.

S Afrose
Bangladesh
Hour 7

The Serene Verse

What a beauty, this art!
Amidst all the serene verses.
Life goes on, losing its rhythms,
That verse acts as a miracle.
This is found in nature's heart,
The most prestigious art on earth.
What a beauty is nature!
Helps to forget the exhausted hut.
Let us follow the ray of hub.
The serene verse is the prominent part.

Elnaz Gorbani
New Zealand
Hour 12

Unification of the soul

Unification of the soul,
a sharing of a story,
our hearts are whole,
to connect is a glory.

A sense of belonging,
a soul's translator,
filled with a longing,

to be part of something greater.

Dave Hirsh
Nassau County, New York
Hour 8

What the _____ Man? Poetry Again

People think that poetry as an art form has died
There is nothing left to say after you get rid of rhythm and rhyme
Stream of consciousness writing creating structural associations

That only the writer, if anyone, truly comprehends (TS Eliot tried to crawl his way out of

      this conundrum or perhaps paradox)

Modernism, post-modernism, surrealism, impressionism, expressionism

      Abstract impressionism, abstract expressionism, realism, super-realism

      Deconstructionism

As analytic devices are fine to comment on other forms of art
But poetry by definition

Needs structure
As certainly maintained by anyone who as ever and only read Trees by Joyce Kilmer

What is poetry after all but words on a page
People think that poetry as an art form has died

As analytic devices are fine to comment on other forms of art
Are the words too hot to touch after prosody has been cancelled (or should we say eliminated,

      or should we say no longer needed once writing was invented)

Have you ever tried to memorize ee cummings

TS Eliot had his comings and goings, and had his women coming and going (was there

      a pun involved?)

Would he really have been happier living at the bottom of the sea?

Jacob Jans
Toronto, Ontario
Hour 7

About that Road Not Taken

Dear Robert,

You never explained what difference it made –
though I can't blame you, the poem

was a joke. The road imagined. You never even took
one step on it. Yet you inspired

generations of shallow-thinking solipsists
to navel gaze down their own fantasy roads–

I can't blame you for that, either, though
you certainly scooted along that academia borne

focus on craft beyond meaning–leading to so
much praise for indecipherable word-play combinations

exclusive to those who dare travel some different
path. Though how could you predict how meaningless

it would all become? Fire and Ice is clever, I'll give you
that. But what was the point of it, really, except

to glorify the obvious? And now, look here, you've
brought me into the fray, folded me like a mute

pigeon into a bag, my words coiffed in the
unbearable influence of your joke–so to those

reading this, please take a moment, ask yourself
what road you really want to be on and why?

And sure, they say the destination is the journey, but
that's only for ineffective drifters–those who see

nothing they want to build, nothing they care
to change, nothing beyond themselves and a damn road.

James Featherstone
Spanish Fork, Utah
Hour 6

Perspective

Perspective, what a thing.

A poem written
during a dark time.

Read by most,
a glimpse into the darkness.

Given to a child,
darkness becomes humor.

Laughter, not sadness.

Smiles, not frowns.

Perspective, what an odd thing.

Manoshi Bose
Mhow, India
Hour 3

Come To Me Like Song

Come to me like a song
a half-remembered melody.
Like promises I half forgot
to a certain special somebody!
Come now to me like my muse
with a tingle and melancholy
a song that tugs at my heartstrings
rekindling pain from bygone follies.

Come to me like an old song
that lifts me into a trance
nudging me from drills of drudgery
to new words and thoughts, perchance!
Come now to me, like my muse.
Save me from dry despair
let my ink flow like tears
my broken wings repair!

Success Koori
Abuja, Nigeria
Hour 12

unseen

in this poem,
there is a fruit screaming onto our tongues,
"taste me."
there is a flower awaiting her maker's
tender touch
there's a book itching to be opened.
i carry my pride on my back
still, the world has refused to cast
even a glare.
in this poem, i am a fading scent
a title that hasn't been read
and if the world doesn't spare
their eyes today
this girl might fade into the page.

Davion Moore
Sandusky, Ohio
Hour 8

The Life of a Writer

I am a writer
trying to find his way

Going through notebook
after notebook
honing my craft

Looking for inspiration
in the smallest things

And then finding the words
to describe them

As nerve-wracking as it can be
I am a writer

Looking for inspiration
And sometimes, finding it
And sometimes, my mind is blank

But that's the beauty of the journey
You keep going

Index of Poets

Abena Ntoso	27
Abioye Aisha	239
Adam Lipscomb	252
Aditi Dixit	76
Aferdita Blaka	192
Aisha Nazir	271
Aishwarya Vedula	65
Aleta D. Nolan	147
Allison Douglas-Tourner	267
Amanda Potter	16
Amber L. Crabtree	107
Amrutha Nair	98
Amy Joy Bostelman	262
Amy Laird	56
Ana Marie Dollano	257
Ananya Panwar	243
Andrew Shaughnessy	177
Angel Rosen	66
Angela L Pantilione	75
Angela Theresa Egic	277
Angie Mountain	158
Anjana Sen	15
Anjum Wasim Dar	144
Anna Cavouras	256
Anne Paterson	218
Anwar Suleman	170
Ariel Westgard	87
Ashay Mathieu	180
Ashley "LuvMiFreely" Powers	35
Ayah April Soliman	131
Bella Ogwuche	290
Betty Jean Steinshouer	148

Name	Page
Bhasha Dwivedi	155
Blessing Omeiza Ojo	90
Bollimuntha Venkata Ramana Rao	150
Bonnie Katzive	230
Brandee Charters	109
Brett Dyer-Bolique and Valkyrie Kerry	116
Brian Hasson	284
Britton Gildersleeve	276
Caitlin Thomson	213
Carol Prost	161
Catherine Dickson	21
Cheryl Mitchell	159
Chidi Nebo	82
Chidozie Chukwubuike	240
Christina Tang-Bernas	238
Chuks Oluigbo	93
Cindy Albers	20
Cindy P. Whitaker	127
Cindy Thompson	22
Colleen Schwartz	184
Confidence Olika	227
Cristy Watson	171
Cynthia Hernandez	97
Dan Tighe	199
Danielle Martin	111
Danielle Wong	105
Darryl Commings	236
Daryl Curnow	216
Daun Wright	115
Dave Hirsh	300
Dave Spinelli	200
David Bruce Patterson	121
David L. Wilson	135
Davion Moore	305
Davita Joie	113
Deanna Ngai	55

Deborah Lynn Dalton aka D², @d2poetry	40
Denise Hill	255
Dexta Jean Rodriguez	149
Diana Kristine	251
Diane Carmony	260
Divya Venkateswaran	139
DJ Delashmit	103
Dominique Russell	229
Donna Meyer	72
DS Coremans	83
Eilidh St John	36
Ekawu Elizabeth Imaji	23
Elijah Kinboade	202
Elizabeth Durusau	102
Elnaz Gorbani	299
Erin Lorandos	176
Ermelinda Makkimane	45
Evelyn Elaine Smith	222
Farzana Suleman	279
Fiona Ryle	43
Francis Muzofa	197
Gabby Gilliam	81
Gena Williams	275
Gina Gil	86
Gita Bharath	246
Given Davis	34
Gopalakrishnan Prakash	201
Gypsie-Ami Offenbacher-Ferris	99
Hafeezah Yates	241
Halle Hund	269
Harvey Schwartz	209
Ian Barkley	52
Ivan Bekaren	108
J R Turek	156
J. Lynn Turney	84

Jacob Jans	301
Jade Walker	47
James Featherstone	302
Jan Meyer	194
Jan Rog	168
Jana O'Dell	100
Janelle Hershberger	274
Janice Mendonca	208
Janis Martin	18
Jarrod Fouts	146
Jennifer Faylor	232
Jessica Leanne Gershon	17
Jill Egland	205
Jill Halasz	129
Jillian Calahan	112
Jo Eckler	185
John Dutton	223
Joshua Factor	62
Joy M. Winstead	266
Joy Miller	160
Joyce Bugbee	77
Julianne Abend	287
Junior Knight	282
Juvairiya Sulthana	191
K. L. Vivian	69
Karen Call	219
Katelyn Dunne	289
Kathleen Tighe	182
Katie Scholan	71
Katrina Moinet	196
Kayla Aldan	106
Kevin J. O'Conner	231
Kristin Cleage	169
KV Adams	283
Lakita Gayden	136
Laura Daniels	179

Lavinia Leon	245
Lee Montgomery-Hughes	32
Leila Tualla	181
Leonora Obed	70
Lesley Tyson	37
Lexanne Leonard	204
Linda Hallstrom	295
Mahima Giri	190
Mandi Smith	92
Manoshi Bose	303
Margarette Wahl	122
Margo Wilson	143
Maria Riofrio	291
Marion Lougheed	217
Maritza M. Mejia	250
Mark Lucker	73
Mary Pecaut	137
Maxine Wise	270
Megan Dausch	26
Megan McDonald	74
Meghana Mandalappu	110
Mel Neet	91
Melissa McCarter	296
Melody Pender	248
Michelle Adegboro	53
Mildred Achoch	297
Momo Campbell	41
Muhammed Ebrahim Suleman	220
Nadiyah Suleiman	215
Nancy Ann Smith	193
Nancy Canyon	261
Nandiya Nyx	24
Nasiha Sadhik	225
Natalie Croney	183
Natasha Vanover	54

Nishant Jain	214
Nykki Norlander	235
Ofuma Agali	19
Oliver McKeithan	203
Pacella Chukwuma Eke	133
Paul Sarvasy	286
Pea Flower Tomioka	211
Preeta Bhuyan	114
Presley Tieman	134
Rarzack Olaegbe	64
Rashmi S Kurup	272
Rebecca Resinski	206
Renae Ogle	280
Renata Pavrey	68
Renee A. Perkins	51
Rhea Kumar	265
River E. Styx	42
Roxann Lawrence	63
Rumbi Chen	278
S Afrose	298
Sabinah Adewole	145
Samantha Carroll	31
Sandra Duncan	33
Sandra Johnson	67
Sandy Lender	264
Sangita Kalarickal Krivosik	195
Sara Anderson	44
Sarah Dittmore	210
Shannon Van	212
Sheila Sondik	221
Shirley Durr	123
Shloka Shankar	189
Shrehya Taneja Delhi, India	263
Silvester Phua	48
Simona Frosin	104
Sincerely BlueJay	25

Solape Adeyemi	244
Starla Tipton	85
Stefanie Hutcheson	253
Success Koori	304
Sue Storts	247
Susan Hannon	178
Tanya LaForce West	224
Tazeen Fatma	242
Teresa Locascio	268
Tessa Mountain	285
Thryaksha	126
Tiffany V. Thomas	288
Tobe T Tomlinson	151
Tonet Rosales	207
Torri Brown	46
Tracy Plath	38
Tricia L. Somers	175
Uditi Naagar	226
V.J.Calone	89
Valarie Kirkwood	258
Vidhi Ashar	167
Vidya Shankar	61
Vijaya Gowrisankar	101
Viswo Varenya Samal	39
Wendie Donabie	259
WREN	88
Zainab Suleiman	273
Zeenat Razzak Shaikh	138